OLD TESTAMENT/*Book of*

JOSHUA

The Battle Begins

Joshua
INDUCTIVE STUDY CURRICULUM

© 2008 Precept Ministries International. All rights reserved.
This material is published by and is the sole property of Precept Ministries International of Chattanooga, Tennessee. No part of this publication may be reproduced, translated, or transmitted in any form or by any means, electronic or mechanical, including photocopying, recording, or any information storage and retrieval system, without permission in writing from the publisher.

Unless otherwise noted, all Scripture quotations are from the New American Standard Bible, ©1960, 1962, 1963, 1968, 1971, 1972, 1973, 1975, 1977, 1995 by the Lockman Foundation, and are used by permission.

Enrichment word definitions are taken with permission from the Merriam-Webster Online Dictionary, © 2005 by Merriam-Webster, Incorporated.

Precept, Precept Ministries International, Precept Ministries International The Inductive Bible Study People, the Plumb Bob design, Precept Upon Precept, and In & Out are trademarks of Precept Ministries International.

978-1-934884-03-4

1st edition
Printed in the United States of America

Table of Contents

Joshua

Intro to Inductive Study................5-8

unit one..9-32
Strong and Courageous
Lesson One	11
Lesson Two	13
Lesson Three	15
Lesson Four	17
Lesson Five	23
Lesson Six	25
Lesson Seven	27

unit two...33-58
Hear, Respond, Remember
Lesson One	35
Lesson Two	37
Lesson Three	39
Lesson Four	41
Lesson Five	43
Lesson Six	45
Lesson Seven	49
Lesson Eight	51

unit three...59-86
Victory and Defeat
Lesson One	61
Lesson Two	63
Lesson Three	65
Lesson Four	69
Lesson Five	71
Lesson Six	77
Lesson Seven	81

unit four...87-114
Our Failures-God's Victories
Lesson One	89
Lesson Two	91
Lesson Three	93
Lesson Four	95
Lesson Five	99
Lesson Six	101
Lesson Seven	105
Lesson Eight	109

unit five...115-141
Obedience Rewarded
Lesson One	117
Lesson Two	121
Lesson Three	125
Lesson Four	127
Lesson Five	129
Lesson Six	131
Lesson Seven	133

unit six..142-172
Laziness, Murder & Responsibility
Lesson One	145
Lesson Two	149
Lesson Three	151
Lesson Four	153
Lesson Five	155
Lesson Six	159
Lesson Seven	161
Lesson Eight	165

unit seven...173-201
The Battle Ends
Lesson One	175
Lesson Two	177
Lesson Three	181
Lesson Four	183
Lesson Five	187
Lesson Six	193
Lesson Seven	195
Lesson Eight	197

appendix...203-286
Observation Worksheets	205
At A Glance Chart	279
Occupying The Land Map	281
Conquering The Land Map	283
About Precept Ministries	285

Joshua

1. Inductive Bible Study - _____

2. There are _____ of Inductive Bible Study:

   a. _____ - _____ ?

   b. _____ - _____ ?

   c. _____ - _____ ?

3. Tools of Observation

   a. The _____ questions

Joshua

b. Mark _____ and _____

c. Make _____

4. Tools of Interpretation

a. _____

_____ ! It rules interpretation.

b. _____

c. _____

5. Application

   a. _____ - resulting in _____

UNIT ONE

Joshua
U-1, Chapter 1

Strong and Courageous

Where are men and women – young and old – who are strong and courageous? How many people do you know that will stand boldly for who they are and what they believe regardless of other people's opinions? Have you ever known someone who gave in to peer pressure instead of risking rejection for doing the right thing? Where are the men and women who know God and believe God even in the midst of trials and conflicts, and are strong enough in character to stand for what God says is true? Are you one of them?

The Book of Joshua tells the story of one man who was strong and courageous – a man singled out by God to lead his generation to victory and holiness. As you study Joshua's life during the next several weeks, you will discover the task God called him to was not without struggle or opposition. How did he stand in the face of opposition? Where did he turn in the midst of trials and conflicts? What did he know about God that gave him the strength and courage he needed to be victorious? God is ready to lead you into victory as well. You, too, can know Joshua's God; think how this knowledge could change your life!

> How many people do you know that will stand boldly for who they are and what they believe regardless of other people's opinions?
>
> Are you one of them?

Whenever you open the Bible, you find yourself face to face with truth. The Bible is not a book of man's private interpretation. Men didn't sit down and think, I'd like to write a book; rather, God sat them down and gave them His words. Second Peter 1:20-21 makes it very clear that the books which comprise the Bible are not a product of human will, rather men were moved by the Spirit of God to write what we now call the Bible. It's really awesome when you think about it – you are about to study the very words of God!

In light of that, the Bible is a book to be approached prayerfully. You want to handle God's Word accurately rather than, as Peter again says in his second epistle, distort it to your own destruction.

This brings us to another reason you need to study it for yourself – there are people who will twist, distort, pervert the Word of God, and use it to manipulate others for their own ungodly purposes. Therefore, when you approach the Word of God to read or study it, it is always wise to ask the Author of the book to help you understand what He has said through those He ordained to record His words.

Remember to always begin each day's study with prayer. You can agree with the following prayer as you begin the study of Joshua's life.

© 2008 Precept Ministries International

Joshua
U-1, Chapter 1

ONE ON ONE: PRAYER

Almighty God, we come to You today as our Elohim, our Creator God. We know that Your Word tells us that You created us for Your pleasure and therefore we want to know what pleases You. We want to understand You and Your ways and live in light of the truth, live **triumphantly.**

We know, Father, that the study of Your Word will not go unchallenged – a hundred distractions, the pressures of our busy lives and even our own laziness can keep us from diligently completing our work each day. Help us not to give up, but finish this study and know the victory of **perseverance**.

O Holy Father, teach us what it is to be strong and courageous. Use this study to deepen our relationship with You and to give us a confidence to stand firm in your truth regardless of the difficult circumstances we encounter. Teach us to live according to the awesome plan you have for us.

We ask this in the name of the One who lives to make **intercession** *for us, Your faithful Son, the Lord Jesus Christ. Amen.*

Now write out below your own prayer – express what you are asking God to do in your life as you study this book.

LESSON ONE

Joshua
U-1, Lesson 1, Chapter 1

HOW IT FITS TOGETHER

1. In order to understand where the book of Joshua fits into the Bible, list which books precede Joshua and draw illustrations of the main events contained in each book. You may remember these from your previous studies or your teacher can help you. For example:

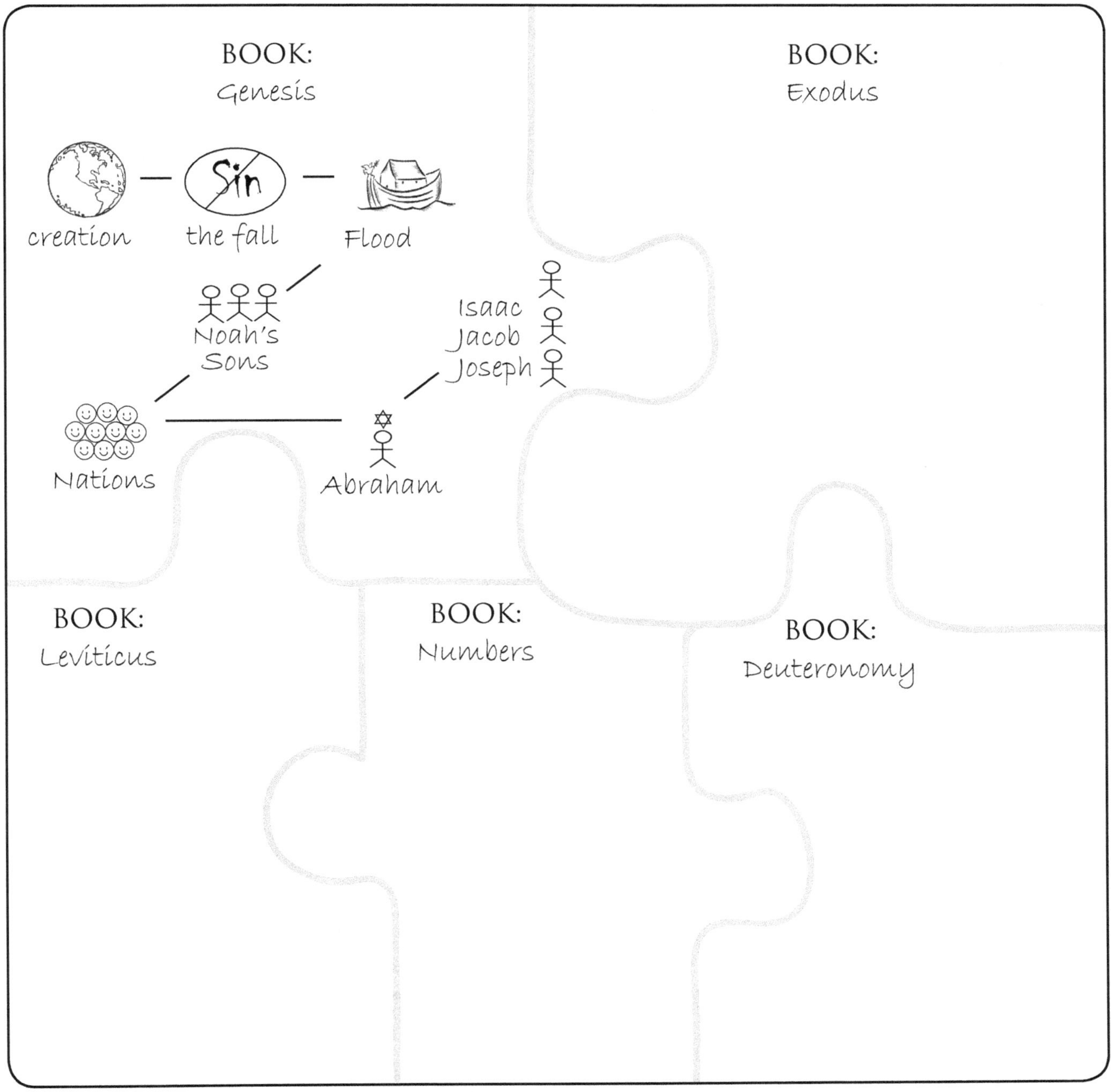

BOOK: Genesis

creation — the fall — Flood
Noah's Sons
Nations — Abraham
Isaac Jacob Joseph

BOOK: Exodus

BOOK: Leviticus

BOOK: Numbers

BOOK: Deuteronomy

Joshua
U-1, Lesson 1, Chapter 1

2. The next thing you want to do as you begin your study is to read through the first chapter of Joshua. The first five books of the Bible, Genesis through Deuteronomy, often referred to as "the Law," include the following major events: Israel's creation as a nation; their **sojourn** and liberation from slavery in Egypt; their journey from Mt. Sinai through the wilderness; and taking possession of the land of **Canaan** under the leadership of Joshua in the book you are studying.

When you finish reading Joshua 1, summarize as briefly as possible what is happening in the chapter. Note the main character(s) and list point by point what happens in this historical account.

MAIN CHARACTERS	MAIN EVENTS
 Who?	What? When?

You're doing great! You've only just begun a journey in God's Word that will teach you many practical things about your relationship with God. Get excited!

LESSON TWO

Joshua
U-1, Lesson 2, Chapter 1

1. Today read through Joshua 1 again and watch for any repeated words or phrases (apart from the names of people) used in this chapter. When you see them, simply write them below.

2. Using your Observation Worksheets located in the Appendix, work through Joshua 1 observing the text and marking the key words or phrases listed below each in its own distinctive way. When you mark key words, also mark any synonyms or pronouns that go with that key word.

   > **Key Word** - A key word is an important word that is repeated for emphasis either in the chapter or throughout a segment of the book, or the entire book.

   Additionally, when you mark key words or phrases, it is always good to color-code the words that are repeated the most rather than simply using a lot of symbols. It doesn't disturb the text as much and makes it easier to identify where that word is used. Use one color or a combination of colors. If you want to distinguish the phrase or the word more, then use a simple diagram such as a cloud like this and then color it.

   Color-coding is an individual thing, as often certain colors represent certain things to an individual. For example, for some yellow is the color used to represent God because God is light; however, others will use purple because it is a royal color. There is no "wrong" way to mark words – simply use what is best for you. However, the workbook will give you suggestions until you are familiar with the process.

   a. *strong* and *courageous*. Try an orange squiggly underline.

   b. *the land* (if it is a reference to the land that God has given to the children of Israel). You will want to mark this phrase throughout the book of Joshua with a green, double underline and shade it blue.

   c. *possess* or *possession*, when it refers to the children of Israel possessing the land given them by God. Color each reference blue.

© 2008 Precept Ministries International

Joshua
U-1, Lesson 2, Chapter 1

    d. *the Lord commanded* or any phrase that is similar with a purple box. This will become an important key phrase you should mark throughout the book of Joshua.

    e. *Joshua* with a blue circle.

    f. geographical locations with a green double underline.

    g. every reference to time, or any words such as *then* or *after* if they indicate an important sequence in events with a green clock.

> How did you do? Did you find all of these key repeated words on your own? Great! If you didn't, don't panic! The more you practice, the better you will get at observing the text carefully!

3. Using a 3x5 notecard make a list of the key words and symbols you have used already. You will add to this card key words you discover in other chapters as we study Joshua.

    EXAMPLE:

LESSON THREE

Joshua
U-1, Lesson 3, Chapter 1

1. Today you are going to do a word study to find the meanings for *strong, courageous,* and *dismayed* in Joshua 1:9 in a Hebrew dictionary if you have the study tools to do so; otherwise your teacher will provide these for you. Record what you learn below.

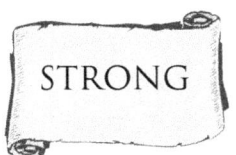

Word Studies - Most of the Old Testament was originally written in Hebrew. By looking up the definitions of these Hebrew words, you can more fully understand the meaning of the text.

2. Whenever you do a word study in the Scripture it is important you take the definition and put it back in the context of the verse. Go back and reread the verses that contained *strong, courageous* and *dismayed.* Think about the definitions you wrote down and answer the following questions:

   a. What does God tell Joshua to be? Use the definitions in your answers.

   Context - the setting or environment in which something is found.

Joshua
U-1, Lesson 3, Chapter 1

b. How will being strong and courageous help Joshua to perform the tasks God has for him?

c. What might cause Joshua to be dismayed and what does God provide to keep him from dismay?

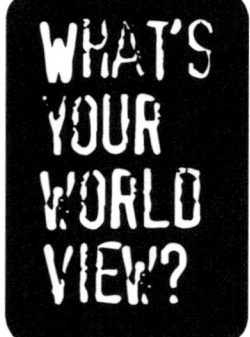

STRONG & COURAGEOUS PROJECT

You've learned about God's definition of strength and courage and His formula for success, but how does the world define and measure these things? For this project you will find out by looking at current newspapers or magazines.

For this project you will need:

One poster board	*Glue*
Various magazines & newspapers	*Scissors*

a. Look through the newspapers and magazines and cut out at least 10 articles, pictures, or advertisements that depict how the world defines strength, courage and success.

b. Type a half-page essay describing what you learned about the world's definitions of these words.

c. Make a collage of the articles, pictures or advertisements and your essay on your poster board.

d. Discuss in class what you found and how the world's view differs from or is similar to what God says.

Isn't it awesome to see what God promised Joshua? God told Joshua what He wanted him to do and then told him how to be successful. Think about the things God has asked you to do — has He given you the same help He gave to Joshua? Do you see how essential God's Word is for believers? And just think... we've only just begun!

LESSON FOUR

Joshua
U-1, Lesson 4, Chapter 1

 1. In the Appendix you will find a chart, "Joshua At A Glance." Record the main theme, the primary subject that is covered in Joshua 1.

2. Now list everything you learned from marking *Joshua* in chapter 1. As you do this, don't miss observing what it will take for Joshua to be strong and courageous. Here are the first few facts to get you started:

JOSHUA

v.1 God speaks to him after the death of Moses
v.1 son of Nun
v.1 servant of Moses
v.2 he is to take this people across the Jordan into the land God had given them
v.3

5 Ws and H - Remember, when making a list, look for the answers to the 5 Ws and H: who, what, when, where, why and how.

© 2008 Precept Ministries International

Joshua
U-1, Lesson 4, Chapter 1

3. Since Joshua is the main character in this book, you need to have some biblical background on this man. How did Joshua come to this significant role in the kingdom of God? What prepared him for leadership?

   Look up the following scriptures and do a character study on Joshua. Look at how he is described (i.e character, age, attitude, etc.); what events he participated in and tasks he performed; and how he is associated with the other people around him.

    As you read these passages, you also need to mark every reference to *the land* the same way you did in Lesson Two when it refers to the land given by God to the children of Israel (Abraham, Isaac and Jacob) since we will do a study of the land later this week. Record what you learn from the text about the land on the chart located on page 26.

   All of this – studying Joshua and the land – is fundamental to understanding the great significance of the book of Joshua, and the picture it gives us as children of God possessing the possessions God has given us. Record what you learn about Joshua in the space below. Here's an example to get you started:

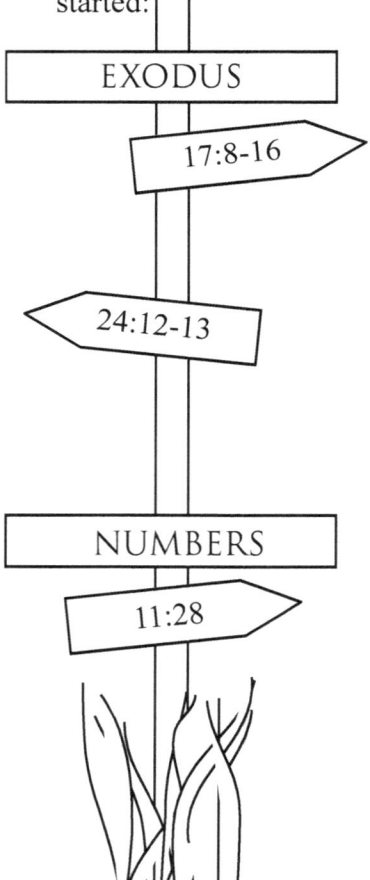

EXODUS

17:8-16 — v.9 told by Moses to choose men to fight against Amalek
v.10 obeyed Moses and fought against Amalek
v. 13 defeated Amalek and his people
v. 14 told by Moses that the Lord will blot out the memory of Amalek from under heaven

24:12-13

NUMBERS

11:28

© 2008 Precept Ministries International

Joshua
U-1, Lesson 4, Chapter 1

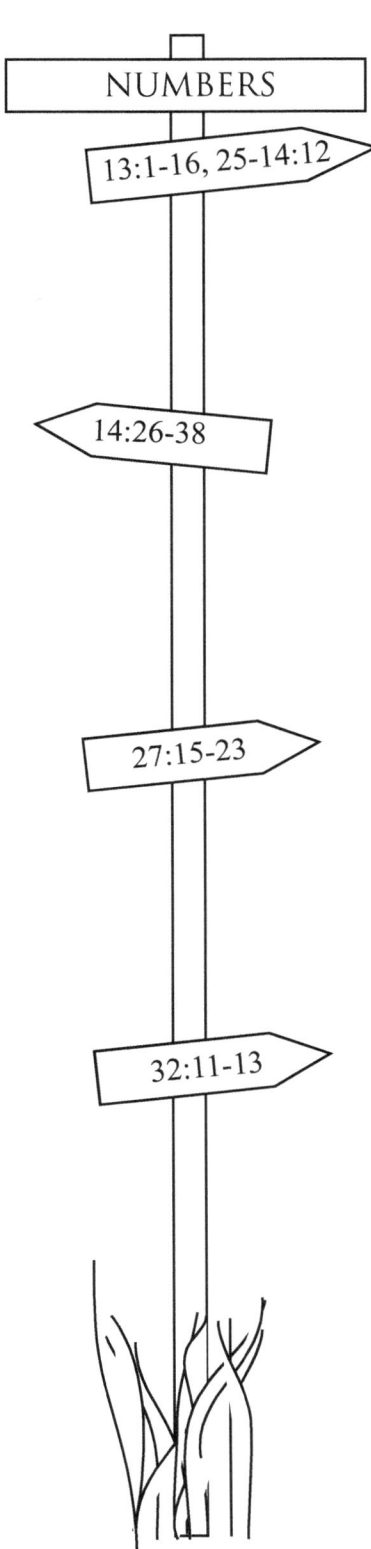

Joshua
U-1, Lesson 4, Chapter 1

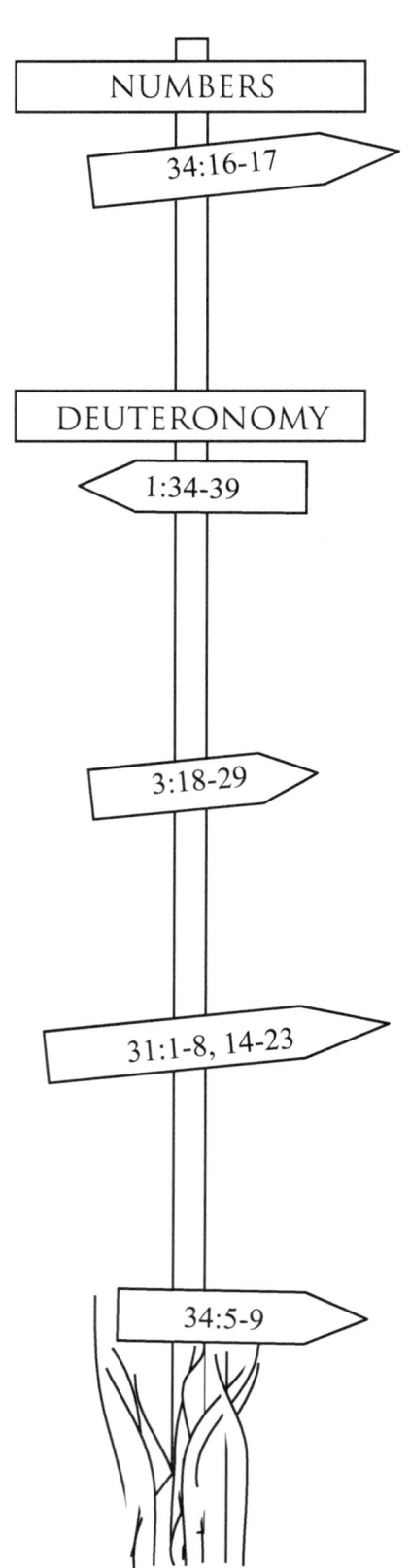

Joshua
U-1, Lesson 4, Chapter 1

4. What key observations of Joshua's life can you apply to your own? Write out your thoughts below.

> There were a lot of Scriptures, weren't there? Yet just think of all you learned about Joshua... and there is so much more to come in the study of this book. When you finish Joshua you will have a thorough knowledge of a man greatly used of God. What lessons for life you are going to learn from this hero of the faith, truths and precepts of life that will set you apart as an example to your friends and family in your beliefs and behavior.
>
> Your generation needs to see **exemplary** followers of Jesus Christ – strong, courageous, and not dismayed by those who hate and deny Jesus Christ and the holiness of God.
>
> Just remember that your study will probably not go unchallenged. The enemy of your soul realizes that the more you know of God's Word and the more you apply His truths, the greater threat you are to his kingdom and his work on this earth.

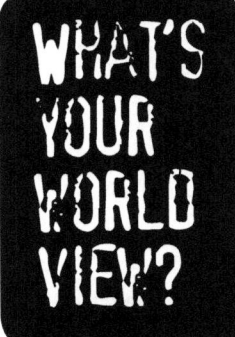

"THE LAND" PROJECT

1. Collect a current event or internet article about the current land disputes in Israel.

2. Write a half-page summary about what land is disputed and who the land belongs to according to Scripture.

© 2008 Precept Ministries International

Joshua
U-1, Lesson 4, Chapter 1

LESSON FIVE

Joshua
U-1, Lesson 5, Chapter 1

Our study in these last lessons of Unit One will focus on the land. If you are really going to appreciate the book of Joshua, understanding what God had to say in respect to the land is crucial.

There is much controversy in our times among the nations of the world as to Israel's right to the land versus the rights of the **Palestinians**. The problem is that many deal with it as political issue rather than a biblical one – which makes it one country's or person's opinion versus another's.

Since the earth is the Lord's and all it contains, and since God appointed our boundaries as the scriptures say, then the answer to whom the former land of Canaan belongs should be found in the Bible. And when we discover what God's Word says, then we should honor God accordingly lest we are found fighting against God. Only the ignorant and fools do that!

> The earth is the Lord's, and all it contains, the world, and those who dwell in it. - Psalm 24:1
>
> "And He made from one, every nation of mankind to live on all the face of the earth, having determined their appointed times, and the boundaries of their habitation." - Acts 17:26

Let's see what God says about this land. It is not only important to our understanding of Joshua, but there's much that is applicable to our personal lives. While the Scriptures we consult will not be all-inclusive since we will only look at the books that precede Joshua, what you observe will provide you with the essence of what God has to say. As you look up these passages, remember that when God makes a **covenant**, He never breaks that covenant.

1. Read through Joshua 1. Note every reference to *the land* and list what you observe about it from these verses.

Joshua
U-1, Lesson 5, Chapter 1

LESSON SIX

Joshua
U-1, Lesson 6, Chapter 1

1. To appreciate what God is saying in Joshua with respect to the land, you need to have a basic understanding of what God said in the **Torah** or Pentateuch, the first five books of the Bible, about the land. As you look up the Scriptures that follow, record your observations on the chart on page 26 entitled "The Land." See if the text gives you any information regarding:

    a. the boundaries and those inhabitating the land before Israel.
    b. who is to possess the land and for how long. Watch for references to descendants.
    c. any conditions in respect to possessing or living in the land.
    d. why the former occupants are being **evicted** and judged.
    e. God's role in the **occupation** of the land.

 As you look up these verses, you will find it beneficial to mark every reference to *the land* in a distinctive way. Also you might mark any references to time with a clock like this: ⏰.

GENESIS
12:1-7
13:12-18
15:7-21
17:1-8
26:1-5
28:1-4, 13-16

EXODUS
6:1,8
23:20-33

LEVITICUS
18:1-3, 24-30
20:22-24
25:1-23
26:1-9

You will find a map at the end of this unit. The location of some of the cities mentioned in the text is not known; however, we have included those of which achaeologists are fairly certain. If you will connect the dots, so to speak, it will give you an idea of the boundaries of the land of Israel's possession.

Leviticus 18 gives instructions to Israel of what behavior would be unacceptable in the land. Does verse 27 give you insight as to why the former inhabitants are being evicted/judged?

NUMBERS
33:40, 50-56
34:1-15

DEUTERONOMY
7:1-6, 16-26
11:8-32
32:8-9
34:1-4

© 2008 Precept Ministries International

25

Joshua
U-1, Lesson 6, Chapter 1

THE LAND

BOUNDARIES/CURRENT INHABITANTS	WHO IS TO POSSESS IT? FOR HOW LONG?
  Where? / Who?	Who? / WHEN? 

CONDITIONS FOR POSSESSING	WHY FORMER INHABITANTS EVICTED/JUDGED	GOD'S PART IN THE OCCUPATION OF THE LAND
 What?	 Why?	 How?

 2. Finally, look on the map on page 29 and mark the boundaries of the land promised to Israel based on the information from your chart.

LESSON SEVEN

Joshua
U-1, Lesson 7, Chapter 1

1. Today, let's take time to go back to God's command to Joshua to be strong and courageous. Some of this will be review but you need to think about this in light of what you learned about God's promises concerning the land. Read Joshua 1 again.

   a. What is Joshua to be strong and courageous about?

   b. Where will his strength and courage come from? How does one become strong and courageous?

   c. How does knowing what God said about the land in Genesis through Deuteronomy help Joshua be strong and courageous? Explain your answer.

2. Look up the following verses written to New Covenant believers and list beside the references anything that might help them be strong and courageous.

© 2008 Precept Ministries International

27

Joshua
U-1, Lesson 7, Chapter 1

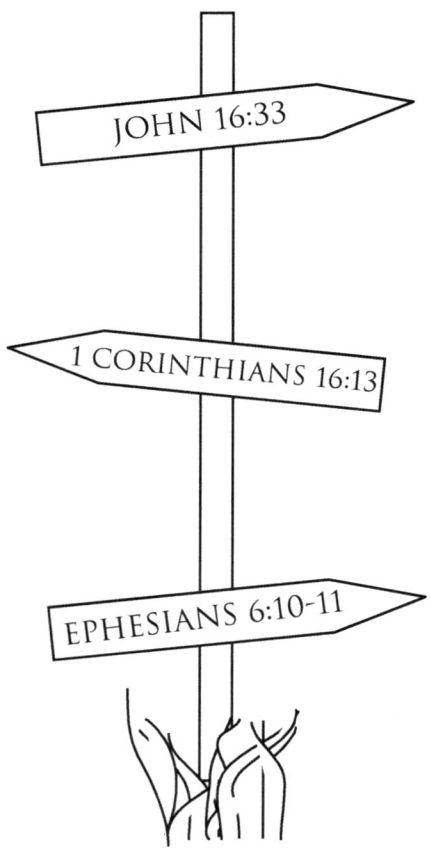

3. Well, faithful one, you are finished and you are to be commended. But before you put down your pen, think about what you learned about God in this unit. You might want to jot it below.

> Do you see how the knowledge you gained can be applied today? To your life personally? Any precepts – standards – which you need to incorporate into your life? Romans 15:4 assures us that what is written for us in the Old Testament is for our instruction, that these Old Testament Scriptures bring us **perseverance** and encouragement and with that hope.

Joshua
U-1, Chapter 1

BORDERS OF THE LAND

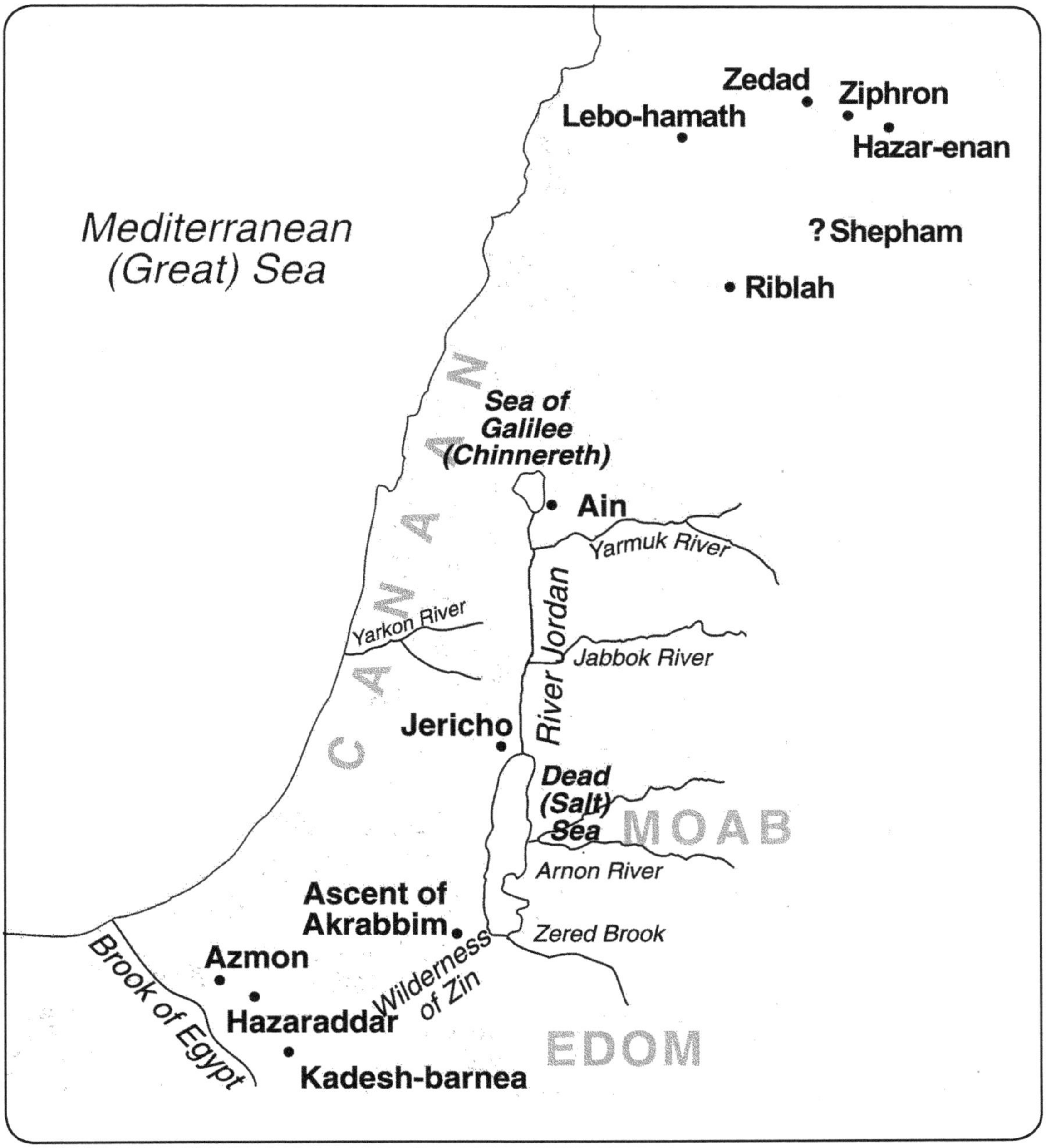

Joshua
U-1, Chapter 1

Joshua
U-1, Chapter 1

ENRICHMENT WORDS

Canaan – the land God gave to Abraham and his descendants.

Covenant – a solemn, binding promise or vow.

Evicted – to force out or expel.

Exemplary – to serve as an example worthy of imitating.

Intercession – to pray or petition God.

Occupation – the possession, use or settlement of the land.

Palestine – the region in ancient Canaan bordering the Mediterranean and East of the Jordan River (not used in the Bible).

Perseverance – to continue in a state of behavior, circumstance or action in spite of opposition or discouragement.

Sojourn – to stay temporarily in a country or region.

Torah – the first five books of the Old Testament.

Triumphantly – to rejoice or celebrate success or victory.

Joshua
U-1, Chapter 1

UNIT TWO

Joshua
U-2, Chapters 2-5

Hear, Respond, Remember

Have you heard about the great things God has done? Scripture records many of the amazing deeds God performed! This unit will focus on the things God did during Joshua's time and their impact on those who heard about them. As you begin this unit, read the following passage from the book of Psalms and think about the responses recorded here to God's great power.

> *When Israel went forth from Egypt,*
> *The house of Jacob from a people of strange language,*
> *Judah became His sanctuary,*
> *Israel, His dominion.*
>
> *The sea looked and fled;*
> *The Jordan turned back.*
> *The mountains skipped like rams,*
> *The hills, like lambs.*
> *What ails you, O sea, that you flee?*
> *O Jordan, that you turn back?*
> *O mountains, that you skip like rams?*
> *O hills, like lambs?*
>
> *Tremble, O earth, before the Lord,*
> *Before the God of Jacob,*
> *Who turned the rock into a pool of water,*
> *The flint into a fountain of water.*
>   *- Psalm 114:1-8*

How does learning about God impact your life? Does it make a difference in the way you live, think or interact with others? Do you confront life's situations and difficulties differently as a result of what you know about God? If even creation responds to God's great power, how much more should we? Think about this and if you have time, discuss it with your instructor before you begin. After you have completed this lesson come back and answer this question again.

Joshua
U-2, Chapters 2-5

Read through the following prayer. Remember your goal in studying God's Word is to KNOW HIM and as a result of knowing Him live differently than those who are **ignorant** of Him and His Word. As you read this prayer you can agree with God that this is the desire of your heart.

ONE ON ONE

*Almighty God, I want to be taught, **reproved**, corrected and trained by your Word so that I might live a life that pleases you. I know there is so much to learn from Your holy Scriptures. I long to know You—to understand Your ways, Your purposes for Your chosen people Israel and for the body of Christ, the church. I want to attain to the fullness of the knowledge of what it means to be strong and courageous and possess all that is mine because I am Yours. I don't want to be fearful of the people or circumstances that surround me. Teach me, as you taught Joshua how to be strong and courageous even when others are not.*

*As I begin my study for this unit, I ask You for **wisdom**, understanding, and the **revelation** of Your Word that I might walk in a manner worthy of my calling as a child of God. I want to be like Joshua who knew what you called him to do and was willing to obey. Open the eyes of my understanding, Father, and show me how to live in the light of Your great power.*

I ask this all in the name of Your Son, Who conquered sin and death and ever lives to make intercession for me. Amen.

Now write out below your own prayer – express what you are asking God to do in your life as you study this lesson.

LESSON ONE

Joshua
U-2, Lesson 1, Chapter 2

1. Key words are words that are repeated for emphasis either in a chapter, throughout a segment of the book, or the entire book. You won't find every word on your bookmark in the chapter you are looking at; just mark the ones you find and any new ones listed for you in the lesson. The directions will help make sure you don't miss the important words for this chapter.

     Read through Joshua 2 on your Observation Worksheets and mark the words on the key word bookmark you began in Unit One. Don't forget to include and/or add:

    a. every reference to *the land*.

    b. every geographical location. The geography is very important in this study. Therefore, as you mark the text, look at the map "Occupying the Land" in the Appendix.

    c. every reference to time.

    d. *Rahab*. Mark her with a pink circle.

    e. every occurrence of *cross* (*crossed*) as it refers to crossing the Jordan River with a black "X" over the word.

    f. any other words you think will help you better understand and remember the context of this chapter. If you find any, decide for yourself how to mark them.

2. List these words, except for Rahab, on your bookmark so that you can watch for them as you continue to study Joshua.

     3. Lastly, record the theme, the primary subject of Joshua 2, on the "Joshua At A Glance" chart you began in Unit One.

Good job! That is enough for today. You may start to think that marking words is boring. But remember, marking words helps you slow down and really see what God is saying. Don't just mark the key words for the sake of marking them. Mark them to unlock the meaning of the text! You can do that by asking the 5Ws and H questions about the words you are marking. Anything that is of real value takes time to achieve. Wouldn't you say understanding God's Word is valuable enough to give it your time.

Joshua
U-2, Lesson 1, Chapter 2

LESSON TWO

Joshua
U-2, Lesson 2, Chapter 2

1. Read through your Observation Worksheet on Joshua 2 again. Note the references to Rahab the **harlot** and make a list of what you learn from the text about her. Here are a few facts to get you started:

   RAHAB

   v.1 a harlot living in Jericho
   v.1 hid two spies sent by Joshua
   v.3 king of Jericho sent word for her to send out the spies
   v.4

© 2008 Precept Ministries International

Joshua
U-2, Lesson 2, Chapter 2

2. Now look up the following references to Rahab. Record what new information you learn about her from these passages. To understand them in context, you may need to read some of the verses before or after the verses listed.

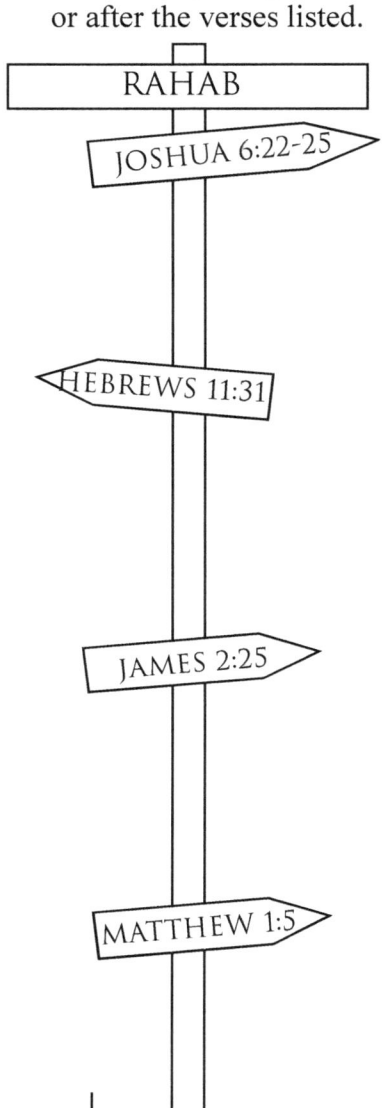

(Although we haven't gotten to this part of the story yet, it is important to see what can be learned about Rahab from the verses at this point.)

Cross references - Sometimes not all the information about one person, event or topic is found in the passage you are studying. Other parts of Scripture give more insight or details. When you look at other parts of the Bible to understand more fully the passage you are studying, you are using Scripture to interpret Scripture. Pretty cool, huh?

Context - Remember! Context is King! It rules interpretation. In order to accurately interpret, or understand the meaning you have to determine the context or setting in which a verse is found.

What do you think about that? Did you look at your enrichment words yet and discover the meaning of the word "harlot?" Think about who Rahab was, what she did and how God used her life. What do you think about who God chooses to use and bless? Think about these things and in the next lesson you will have a chance to think about how these truths apply to your life.

LESSON THREE

Joshua
U-2, Lesson 3, Chapter 2

Today you are going to take all that you have learned about this biblical character Rahab and think about why God has included her story in Scripture. Now that you know what the Bible says about Rahab you need to think about why her story is important to your life.

1. Why do you think God included the story of Rahab's life – what is important for you to understand about her and God's dealings with her?

> **Transformation** is the goal of all Bible study, which happens through **application** of God's Word. You don't want to just know what the Bible says, or even just what it means, you want to know how the meaning of God's Word applies to your life. In other words, how does knowing and understanding God's Word change how you think or live?

2. Are there any applications from Rahab's life – any lessons that you can apply to your life? Can you identify with Rahab in any way? Have you ever done anything, which would make you think God could never use you?

3. If God is the same yesterday, today and forever (as His Word says He is) what kind of people can God use and bless?

4. How would knowing these truths about Rahab and God help you encourage someone else? What would you say to someone who thought they had made too many mistakes or were too "messed up" to ever be wanted or used by God?

© 2008 Precept Ministries International

Joshua
U-2, Lesson 3, Chapter 2

5. Finally, how did Rahab respond to the stories of God's great power? How did the other people respond? How do you respond when you hear of God's mighty works and His great power?

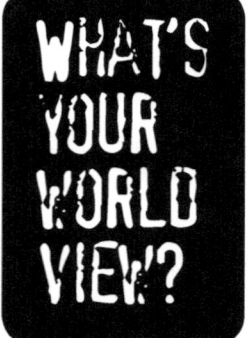

FAITH OR FEAR? - PROJECT

For this project you will need:

Poster board   *Magazines*   *Glue*
Scissors   *Internet*   *Newspapers*

Think about a recent world crisis people clearly saw God's part in. Find a printed or internet article about the crisis. Think about it, talk to adults in your life and ask them how people responded to the events. Compare their reaction to Rahab's response to the events she learned about and how the other people of the land responded.

After you have gathered your information take a poster board and use half of it to depict how people like the inhabitants of the land responded to God's mighty works and great power, and the other half to depict how Rahab and people like her respond. Be creative, you can use pictures from magazines, words or drawings to illustrate your points.

LESSON FOUR

Joshua
U-2, Lesson 4, Chapters 3-4

1. Read through Joshua 3 and 4 on your Observation Worksheets and mark the words on your key word bookmark. Don't forget to include and/or add:

    a. references to time.

    b. geographical locations especially *Jordan*.

    Observation – What does it say?!

    c. any other key words or phrases from your bookmark that are in this chapter.

    d. every reference to the *ark of the covenant*. Decide for yourself or with your instructor how to mark it. You will want to mark it the same way throughout Scripture as it is very important and repeated in the Old Testament.

When you read these chapters, think about how incredible this event is in the history of Israel. Note how God is referred to in Joshua 3; observe His mighty acts.

2. Since the *ark* plays a central role in these chapters, list the main things you learned from marking the references to it.

Lists - Make lists by answering the 5Ws and H questions. Do you learn anything about the ark? What they are doing with the ark? Who was to do what with it? Where was it going? Why? When? How? What was the result, etc.

© 2008 Precept Ministries International

41

Joshua
U-2, Lesson 4, Chapters 3-4

3. Record what the ark represented according to this passage in Exodus. (You don't need to list all the details about the ark – only what is most important.)

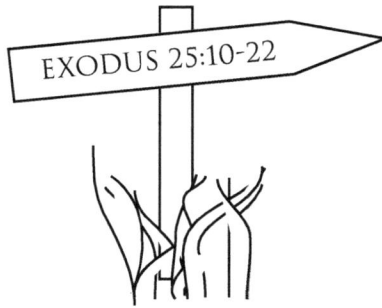

Wow! Talk about God's great power!! How does it make you feel to know that you serve a God with this much power!

LESSON FIVE

Joshua
U-2, Lesson 5, Chapters 3-4

1. Think about what you learned from chapter 1 about God's part in the occupation of the land. If necessary, go back and read chapter 1 again. Think about what you learned about the ark. Why do you think God had the ark leading the people?

2. According to Joshua 3:9-13, how would the people know that God was among them and would do what He promised? Did it happen?

3. Why do you think God gave them this sign? What does that tell you about God?

 4. Briefly list the main events of Joshua 4. (We will talk more about these events at the end of the unit.) Look at the map at the end of this unit to see where these events are taking place.

 5. Record the theme of Joshua 3 and 4 on the " Joshua At A Glance" chart.

Joshua
U-2, Lesson 5, Chapters 3-4

LESSON SIX

Joshua
U-2, Lesson 6, Chapter 5

1. Read Joshua 5 on your Observation Worksheets and mark the words on your key word bookmark. Don't forget to include or add:

    a. every reference to *circumcision*.

    b. *manna*. Although it is only used twice in this chapter it would be good to mark it so that you don't miss what happens with it.

2. List below or in the margin of your Observation Worksheet next to the appropriate verses the main events in this chapter.

> You are familiar enough now with marking to come up with your own way to mark these words. If you need help ask your instructor. Occasionally, the directions will give you suggestions on how to mark a word. Remember, there is no right, wrong or "holy" way to mark words ☺ Just remember not to mark all the words the same way - that defeats the purpose!

3. Record the theme of Joshua 5 on the "At A Glance" chart.

4. What do you learn from Joshua 5 about circumcision? Use the 5 Ws and an H.

© 2008 Precept Ministries International

Joshua
U-2, Lesson 6, Chapter 5

> At this point you may be thinking, "Yuck! Why do we have to learn about this?" Just remember, "For whatever was written in earlier times was written for our instruction, so that through perseverance and the encouragement of the Scriptures we might have hope" (Romans 15:4). We need to know these truths in order to understand God and His great plan for the ages, which would include you as a believer.

5. Why was circumcision so important? Look up the following verses and write down what you learn about circumcision from the text. You may want to mark circumcision in your Bible.

 *(This is the first time circumcision is mentioned in the Bible)*

Joshua
U-2, Lesson 6, Chapter 5

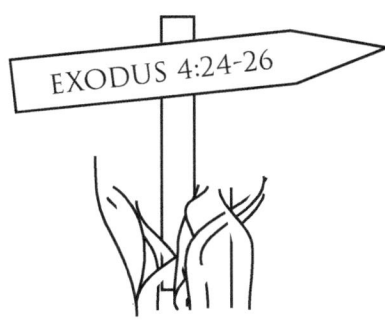

6. Now can you see the significance of what's happening in Joshua 5? These men are being circumcised in fulfillment of God's covenant! Consider where geographically this event takes place. Look at the map at the end of this unit to help you answer the following questions.

   a. Which side of the Jordan are the people on when they are circumcised?

   b. Where are their enemies?

   c. Are they able to go to war if their enemies attack right after they have been circumcised? Why or why not?

   d. Why then do you think God asked them to do this right before going into battle? Think about what you learned in chapter 1 about God's part in taking the land.

7. How **dependent** do you think God wants you to be on him? How important is obedience to God? Write out your thoughts on circumstances God can use or has used in your life to remind you to obey and depend on Him.

© 2008 Precept Ministries International

Joshua
U-2, Lesson 6, Chapter 5

LESSON SEVEN

Joshua
U-2, Lesson 7, Chapters 3-5

God told Joshua that He would be with him even as He had been with Moses (Joshua 1:5) and that he was to be strong and courageous and do according to all the law that Moses had commanded.

1. Read through Joshua 3–5 again. Ask yourself questions about Joshua's leadership such as: How did he lead? What was his attitude? Where did he get his authority from? What was Joshua's **motive** for leading? etc.

    If you already completed the study on Moses you may remember what you learned about his leadership. Do you see any parallels between Moses and Joshua? If so, what are they? Record them in the appropriate columns on the chart below.

    Don't imagine or add anything to the text, simply take your insights from the text rather than your imagination. If you have not studied Exodus, then simply list the main things Joshua does in these chapters and leave the part about Moses blank.

MOSES	JOSHUA

© 2008 Precept Ministries International

49

Joshua
U-2, Lesson 7, Chapters 3-5

2. Are you in a role of leadership? If you are a big brother or big sister, then you are! If you are older than some of the students in your class, youth group or community, then you are! If you are on a student council, part of a sports team or musical group, then you are!

   From seeing the examples of these two leaders, what can you apply to your own life? How did they lead? How can you learn to lead as they did?

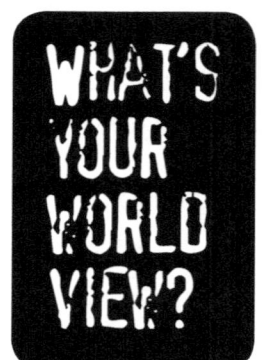

GODLY LEADERSHIP PROJECT

What makes a good leader according to the world? What traits or qualities make them admirable? What do you see about leaders today that contrast what you learned about Joshua and Moses? Write a two-paragraph essay that explains the contrasts. Conclude your essay by describing what you will look for in those you follow based on what you've learned.

You can gather your information either from your own observations or by getting the insights of adults in your life.

LESSON EIGHT

Joshua
U-2, Lesson 8, Chapters 1-5

1. When you study Scripture you always should ponder what you learned about God. God's Word reveals who He is. We must know who He is if we are going to love, honor and obey Him. What have you learned about God from these first five chapters of Joshua? Write out your insights below. Then think how such knowledge might help you in your day-to-day life.

INSIGHTS ABOUT GOD	HOW THIS CAN HELP ME

2. In Joshua 4, God instructs the people to choose one man from every tribe to carry a stone from the middle of the Jordan to set up as a **memorial**.

   a. Go back to Joshua 4 and observe the purpose in all this. Record it below.

Joshua
U-2, Lesson 8, Chapters 1-5

b. As you read through the Word of God, you will find God's people setting up memorials of significant acts and works of God, or naming places and children according to the events. These "memorials" serve as signposts in the life of a family or nation – reminders of significant events or times in our personal history. "Sayings," "words of wisdom," and insights you share with *your* children can do the same.

Ask God to show you memorials you can set up and share with your family and friends and even pass on to your future children. List these to remember what God showed you.

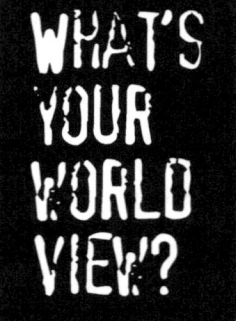

MEMORIAL STONE PROJECT

For this project you need:

1 medium-sized rock (big enough to write a sentence or two)
Permanent marker

Memorialize something that God has done in your life by writing it on a rock to remember and pass on to generations to come. If you are a member of a class, bring this to class to share with the other students. Then set up a place for everyone to keep their rocks to see daily throughout the rest of your study on Joshua and remember what God has done for you and others.

If you are studying this on your own share this with your family or friends. Put your rock in a significant place in your house where you will see and remember what God has done for you.

Joshua
U-2, Lesson 8, Chapters 1-5

This is the end of Unit Two! You have been diligent and disciplined to get each day's work completed. Hasn't it been worth it? And just think—this is work which will benefit you not only for the rest of your life, but also for eternity. If you will treasure these truths in your heart and allow God to cause them to change how you live, you too can be a leader like Joshua and bring honor to God.

Joshua
U-2, Lesson 8, Chapters 1-5

Joshua
U-2, Chapters 2-5

CROSSING THE JORDAN

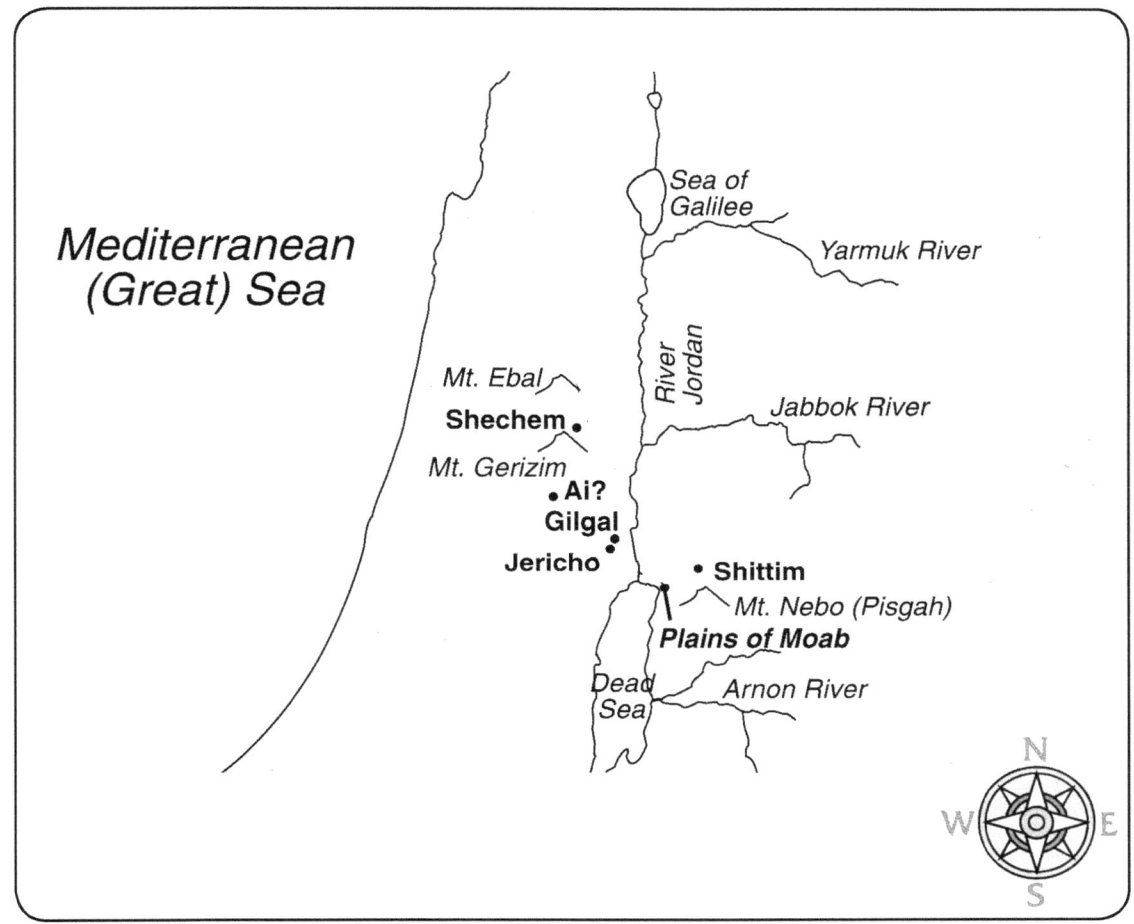

Joshua
U-2, Chapters 2-5

Joshua
U-2, Chapters 2-5

ENRICHMENT WORDS

Dependent – relying on another for support.

Dominion – supreme authority; absolute ownership.

Geography – a science that deals with the locations on and the description of the earth's surface.

Harlot – female prostitute.

Ignorant – lacking knowledge or comprehension of the thing specified; unaware, uninformed.

Memorial – something that keeps remembrance alive.

Motive – something (as a need or desire) that causes a person to act.

Reproved – to be shown they are wrong.

Revelation – an act of communicating divine truth; making known what was hidden or unknown.

Wisdom – knowledge rightly applied.

Precept Upon Precept

Joshua
U-2, Chapters 2-5

UNIT THREE

Joshua
U-3, Chapters 6-8

Victory and Defeat

*Oh give us help against the adversary,
For deliverance by man is in vain.*

*Through God we will do valiantly;
And it is He who shall tread down our adversaries.
- Psalm 108:12-13*

Joshua and the battle of Jericho – a story you have probably heard many times. You may even recall songs you sang when you were very young about this historic event. The question we want to focus on in this unit is – why? Why is this story so popular? Why is this story so important? And, how will fully understanding this **narrative** change how you think or live? Is the story of the battle of Jericho just a children's story like any other or are there truths about who God is and how to trust Him even when He asks us to do something that may seem ridiculous?

Begin this unit with prayer and ask God to allow His Holy Spirit to answer these questions and more as you study each lesson.

ONE ON ONE:

*Father, as we begin our studies this week, we come to You again because You are our very life — our wisdom, our shield, our protector, the **redeemer** and defender of our lives. Like the children of Israel, we face enemies of unrighteousness, ungodliness — people who do not know You either out of ignorance or willful rejection. Help us, Father, to walk in victory — to be strong and courageous and not dismayed. Show us how to deal with them so that we walk under Your clear orders and leadership.*

Teach us Your precepts of life as we study; for, Father, we so long to be workmen who will not be ashamed when we see You face-to-face.

Thank You, Father, for our Captain of Hosts who sits at Your right hand of power, for it is through His total conquest of sin at Calvary that we come into Your presence to ask these things. Amen.

Joshua
U-3, Chapters 6-8

Write out a prayer of your own expressing to God your desire to diligently study these chapters and understand the truths contained within.

LESSON ONE

Joshua
U-3, Lesson 1, Chapter 6

1. Before you begin observing Joshua 6, write out below everything you remember about Joshua and the battle of Jericho. At the end of this unit, come back to this question and see how much you got right and if there were any new details you discovered as you looked more closely at the biblical account.

> Read with a purpose! Don't forget that observation is not a mindless assignment. You need to train yourself to THINK as you read. You do not want to just skim or scan the text. You want to closely examine it to see what it is really saying so that you will be able to accurately interpret or understand what it means. Your goal is to accurately understand the meaning of the text so that you can accurately apply God's truth to your life.
>
> Begin your study of this narrative by observing Joshua 6. As you read through Joshua 6, capture the scene in your mind. Imagine what this sight must have looked like—to those looking down from the walls of Jericho and to those marching silently around them, day after day.

2. As you mark key words listed on your bookmark, also mark every reference to *under the ban*. Also don't forget the references to *the ark of the covenant* and to time.

3. Add *under the ban* to your key word bookmark.

4. When you finish your observations, once again list below or in the margin of the text the progression of events as they occur in this chapter.

© 2008 Precept Ministries International

Joshua
U-3, Lesson 1, Chapter 6

5. Finally, record the theme of Joshua 6 on the "Joshua At A Glance" chart.

> Did you learn anything new so far? If so, wasn't it exciting to see more to the story than just the details you learned when you were very small? The Bible says there is a time for young believers to grow up in all aspects and to mature to the point of no longer needing the elementary teachings of the Word, but also a time to begin partaking of the meat of the Word (Ephesians 4:14, 15 and Hebrews 5:12-14, 6:1). You are maturing physically, emotionally and mentally already... isn't it time to mature spiritually as well?!

LESSON TWO

Joshua
U-3, Lesson 2, Chapter 6

> "All Scripture is inspired* by God and profitable for teaching, for reproof, for correction, for training in righteousness;"
> – 2 Timothy 3:16
>
> "For no prophecy was ever made by an act of human will, but men moved** by the Holy Spirit spoke from God."
> – 2 Peter 1:21

God moved the author of Joshua to purposely unfold the events and instructions from Him through His servant Joshua to the children of Israel in a very specific way. No word of God, no account, is of man's human interpretation; Scripture was written by men moved by God. These are God-breathed words. Therefore it is even important to watch the order in which things are recorded.

* The word "inspired" is literally "God-breathed," *theopneustos*.

Take a few minutes and read through Joshua 5 and 6. As you read watch the way the content of these chapters unfolds. In other words, look at the order of the events in these two chapters.

** The word "moved" means to bear or carry, signifying that these men were borne along by the Holy's Spirits power, not by their own will or thoughts, *phero*.

When you finish, think about the following questions. Although you may not be able to answer all of them at this point in your study, jot down any thoughts or insights that come to mind.

1. Why did the events that took place at Gilgal in chapter 5 need to happen before the events at Jericho in chapter 6? Think about what you learned concerning the significance of circumcision in Unit Two.

© 2008 Precept Ministries International

Joshua
U-3, Lesson 2, Chapter 6

2. What did you see in Unit Two about the role of the ark of the covenant?
3. Why do you think God instructed the Israelites to carry it around the city of Jericho?

4. What is its position in the march? Why would it be placed there?

5. Draw a picture in the appropriate column depicting the placement of the ark in relation to the people when Israel crossed the Jordan and when they circled Jericho.

CROSSING THE JORDAN	JERICHO

> Do you see the importance of knowing God's instructions and following them explicitly? God doesn't always ask us to do something the same way twice. It is important that we always ask Him for direction and obey Him completely. Proverbs 3:5-6 says, "Trust in the Lord with all your heart and do not lean on your own understanding. In all your ways acknowledge Him, and He will make your paths straight." We may not always understand His instructions, but we should always follow them.

LESSON THREE

Joshua
U-3, Lesson 3, Chapter 6

Continue observing and interpreting Joshua 6 by answering the following questions:

1. Why are events interrupted in Joshua 6:17-19? What instruction or warning does Joshua give to the people?

   Interpretation – What does the text mean? Observation lays a solid foundation for accurately interpreting God's Word.

2. What happens to anyone who does not obey this warning?

3. What happens to the wall? According to the text, is there any significance in the way it falls?

4. What have you learned from chapter 6 that you can apply to your life? Think about this and answer it below before you move on to the next question.

   Learn how to apply God's Word to your life – prayerfully ask God to reveal to you how the truths you saw can make a difference in your day-to-day living. You won't always have a workbook that will ask you application questions.

© 2008 Precept Ministries International

Joshua
U-3, Lesson 3, Chapter 6

5. Does God still give instructions that we are to carry out today? List two or three of the instructions God has given to believers.

6. Do you follow God's instructions carefully and completely, or do you pick and choose what and when you will obey Him? How should you obey Him?

7. How does knowing that God is powerful enough to bring down the walls of Jericho help you trust Him with difficult circumstances in your own life?

8. Do the instructions God gave Israel concerning Jericho seem a little silly or unreasonable? Do you think it made sense to the people that they were going to conquer a fortified city just by marching around it and then shouting at the walls? Have you ever felt like God's instructions to you were "silly" or didn't make sense? What can you learn from chapter 6 that will help you overcome your doubt?

Joshua
U-3, Lesson 3, Chapter 6

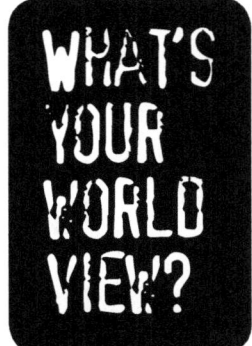

THE WALLS COME TUMBLING DOWN – PROJECT

1. Think about your own life and how God may have caused "walls" to come tumbling down. Have you ever obeyed God and seen Him miraculously move obstacles to give you victory? Maybe He asked you to forgive someone and He restored a relationship that you thought could never be mended. Perhaps He asked you to take on a challenge you thought you would never succeed at that you overcame.

Write out a paragraph essay describing what God asked you to do, how you obeyed and what was the result.

What an amazing God you serve! He can cause the walls of a city to fall flat! Is anything impossible for God? Do you know Him well enough and trust Him enough to obey Him even when it seems He's asking you to shout at a wall and watch it fall down?

Joshua
U-3, Lesson 3, Chapter 6

LESSON FOUR

Joshua
U-3, Lesson 4, Chapter 7

1. Read Joshua 6:17-7:26 to put yourself in context. When you finish, do your observations on Joshua 7. As you continue to mark key words, don't forget to mark:

    a. occurrences of *under the ban* as you did in Joshua 6.

    b. references to *covenant*. This is a word you should habitually mark as you read through the Bible because everything God does is based on covenant. God is the **sovereign** administrator of all covenants. If they are broken, He becomes the **arbitrator**, for a covenant is a solemn binding agreement.

    c. *sinned* and any form of the synonym *transgression* in the same way.

    d. *consecrate* (although it is only used two times in this chapter and three times total in the book of Joshua, mark it in this chapter and in Joshua 3:5).

2. Add these words to your key word bookmark.

3. Once again list the main events in Joshua 7. Record them below or on the Observation Worksheet.

4. Record the main theme of Joshua 7 on the "At A Glance" chart.

© 2008 Precept Ministries International

69

Joshua
U-3, Lesson 4, Chapter 7

LESSON FIVE

Joshua
U-3, Lesson 5, Chapters 6 & 7

What was so terrible about what Achan did? What does it mean for something to be *under the ban*? In this lesson you will look at this incident more closely to understand more fully the terrible consequences of ignoring God's warnings.

1. Do a word study on this phrase as it is used in Joshua 6 and 7. Make sure you write out the Hebrew word and the definition.

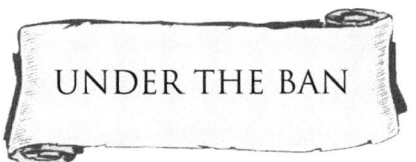

> **Word studies** and cross-references help us to understand the meaning and interpretation of the text.

2. Now take the definition and put it back in the context of the events taking place in chapters 6 and 7. Think about the definition and answer the following questions.

   a. What was to be *under the ban*? What was to happen to it?

   b. What happens if the people don't keep themselves from the things *under the ban*?

   c. What happened to Israel as a result of Achan ignoring God's instruction and warning?

© 2008 Precept Ministries International

Joshua
U-3, Lesson 5, Chapter 7

3. The phrase *under the ban* is used only in Deuteronomy and Joshua. Look up the following Scriptures observing where it falls in the text. Record what you learn from looking at these cross-references.

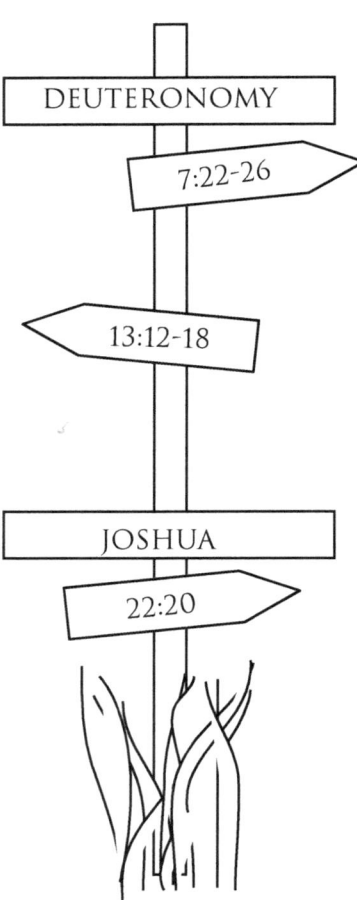

4. What do you learn from marking *sin* (transgression)?

Joshua
U-3, Lesson 5, Chapter 7

5. Read through Joshua 7:1-26.

   a. What were the people told to do?

   b. *Consecrate* means to be set apart, to purify or make clean. What would Achan and his family have needed to do to consecrate themselves?

   c. What did you learn about Achan's sin just from observing the text?

   d. What led him to disobey God?

   e. How did it come about?

© 2008 Precept Ministries International

Joshua
U-3, Lesson 5, Chapter 7

f. What were the **consequences**? Whom did it affect?

g. Do a word study on this word from Joshua 7:21.

h. Put the definition of this word back into the context and explain in your own words what Achan did that led him to sin.

i. Were the things Achan desired worth the consequences?

> Have you ever considered the story of Achan before you made a decision you knew was against the clear teaching or character of God? Have you ever wanted something so badly you knowingly disobeyed your parents in order to get it? Was the thing you desired worth the consequences you suffered? Is it ever? What will you do the next time you desire something you know you are not allowed to have? Will you choose to ignore God's commands and accept the consequences, even if that means innocent people suffer so you can satisfy yourself?
>
> Maybe you know how it feels to suffer the consequences of someone else's sin. Maybe you suffer because of a decision your parents, another adult, or even a friend made that was clearly contrary to God's commands. Do you want to cause someone else the kind of pain you have suffered?
>
> Ask God to help you remember to consider the consequences before you make a choice that can lead to pain not only in your life but in another's as well.

Joshua
U-3, Lesson 5, Chapter 7

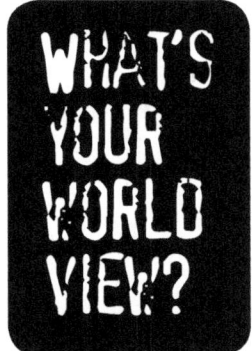

SIN AND CONSEQUENCES - PROJECT

For this project you will need:

Newspapers   *Magazines*   *Internet*
Scissors   *Glue*

Have the consequences of your sin ever affected other people? Do you see people sinning today and other people suffering because of those choices? Find an article from a newspaper, magazine or the internet that describes someone's actions that are clearly contradictory to God's commands and how other's suffered from the consequences of their sin.

To help you get started think about this: Do nations suffer because leaders make bad choices? Do children suffer when parents make bad choices? Do parents suffer when children make bad choices?

Once you find an article, cut or print it out, and paste it to a piece of paper. Then write out below the article or on the back of the page the sin that was committed and the consequences that were suffered.

Example:

```
┌─────────────────────────────────────┐
│      ┌─────────────────────┐        │
│      │      ARTICLE        │        │
│      └─────────────────────┘        │
│                                     │
│       SIN      CONSEQUENCES         │
│                                     │
│                                     │
│                                     │
└─────────────────────────────────────┘
```

© 2008 Precept Ministries International

Joshua
U-3, Lesson 5, Chapter 7

LESSON SIX

Joshua
U-3, Lesson 6, Chapter 7

Too often in today's culture we live for today, "in the now," thinking only of ourselves and the things that bring us pleasure. Too many young people make decisions without ever considering how the choices they make today will affect not only their future, but the lives of their future spouses and children. Think about the numerous parents whose children suffer from diseases because they chose to disobey God when they were young and have sex with whoever, whenever they wanted. Think about the young people just like you who spend their youth in reform schools or even die because they chose to do what they wanted and ignore any and all authority.

Do you think their parents and siblings suffered as a result? Because this is such an important topic for you to understand, you will continue in this lesson to look at other people in the Bible who sinned and the consequences others suffered as a result.

1. Read Genesis 3:1-7 and 2 Samuel 11:1-6; 12:9-12. Compare this with what you just learned about Achan and his sin.

   a. Fill in the chart below with the information you get from these passages. How did Adam and David's sin follow the same pattern you saw in Achan? The column for Achan has already been filled in.

	ACHAN	ADAM	DAVID	ME
PATH TO SIN:	Saw the mantle, silver and gold Coveted them Took them Hid them under his tent			
CONSEQUENCES	Death for him, his family, and all that belonged to him			

© 2008 Precept Ministries International

Joshua
U-3, Lesson 6, Chapter 7

> Does death still happen as a result of sin today? We know as a believer that Christ died on our behalf so that we would no longer be dead spiritually, but can we still experience "death" as a consequence for our sin? Have you ever experienced the "death" of certain privileges, friendships or trust as a result of your sin? Sadly, you or someone else could die physically as a result of your sin. Can you think of sins leading to physical death as a result of something you did? It is important to remember that sin always costs us something, and it will always cost you more than you expect to pay.

b. Now fill in the last column. Can you think of a time you followed the same path to sin and suffered consequences as a result? Fill in the chart under "Me" with the details.

c. According to this passage (EPHESIANS 4:22-32), what are some things we should "lay aside" or put "under the ban" today?

2. Although we experience consequences as a result of our sin, is that the end of the story or is there hope?

a. What do we need to do? (1 JOHN 1:9-10)

b. What will Jesus do for us as a result?

Joshua
U-3, Lesson 6, Chapter 7

> Do you think others need to know about the consequences of sin? You need to understand and heed these warnings you learned from Achan's life, but you also need to share these truths with others. Ask God for the opportunity to share them—and when it comes, be strong and courageous. Don't be dismayed by their faces!

Joshua
U-3, Lesson 6, Chapter 7

LESSON SEVEN

Joshua
U-3, Lesson 7, Chapter 8

1. You have come to the final chapter of study for this unit. Once again you need to observe the text so you can discover what God's Word says. Going through this exercise will not only help strengthen the habit of seeing exactly what the text says, it will also enable you to better understand and remember what it says.

    When you observe Joshua 8, mark any key words you have on your bookmark along with geographical locations and references to time. Also mark *ambush* and *commanded*.

2. Now look at every place you marked *commanded* and list what you learn. Be sure to ask the 5 Ws and an H.

3. Read through Joshua 8 again, noting the occurrences of *ambush*. Ambush means "to lurk." Draw the strategy God gave Joshua for taking the city of Ai in the space below.

© 2008 Precept Ministries International

Joshua
U-3, Lesson 7, Chapter 8

4. Locate Mt. Ebal and Mt. Gerizim on the map "Occupying the Land" located in the Appendix. Note the relationship of these mountains to the cities of Gilgal, Jericho, and Ai.

   a. List below the details of what happens at these two mountains and why.

   b. Now compare this with the following passage. What does this tell you about Joshua and his leadership? And does it give you any further insight into what occurred in Joshua 8:30-35?

   DEUTERONOMY 27

5. Finally considering these three chapters, Joshua 6, 7, and 8, what have you learned that you can apply to your life?

   a. What knowledge have you gained that can help you walk in a way that is pleasing to God?

   b. What have you learned about God from these chapters?

Joshua
U-3, Lesson 7, Chapter 8

c. Have you learned anything about leadership? Think about how Joshua dealt with defeat and with the sin of Achan. Does a leader ignore failure or learn from it? Does a leader ignore sin or deal with it?

d. Why do you think Joshua 6 is such a **captivating** story?

e. Is there anything new you learned from this study that you didn't know before about the fall of Jericho? What is it? Why do you think you saw it this week for the first time?

6. Record the theme of chapter 8 on the "At A Glance" chart.

> You have done it – completed another unit in the book of Joshua! Just remember there's more land to conquer and more of God's great power and mighty works to examine.

Joshua
U-3, Lesson 7, Chapter 8

Joshua
U-3, Chapters 6-8

ENRICHMENT WORDS

Arbitrator – one who decides or determines between choices.

Captivating – influencing and dominating by some special charm, art, or trait and with an irresistible appeal.

Consequences – the outcome or result of actions or choices.

Explicitly – leaving no question as to meaning or intent.

Narrative – the retelling of an event or story.

Redeemer – a person who purchases freedom for a slave by payment of ransom.

Sovereign – one that exercises supreme, permanent authority.

Joshua
U-3, Chapters 6-8

UNIT FOUR

Joshua
U-4, Chapters 9-12

Our Failures - God's Victories

Do you trust God? Why or why not? How do you know whether you can trust someone? You probably answered, "Because you know them and they have proven they are trustworthy."

If your answer to the first question was "no," then think about these questions: Have you ever gotten to know God? Do you know the reasons why He is trustworthy? Do you think it would be beneficial to know and trust someone who would never let you down and who would never go back on His word or promises? And who always has your best interest at heart?

If you answered "yes" to the first question, how have you demonstrated in your day-to-day living that you trust God? How would other people, by looking at your life, know that you believe in God? Do you trust God enough to obey Him even when others mock you? Do you trust God enough to wait for or even give up something you want when He says "no?" Do you trust God enough to allow Him to lead and direct your life, your friendships, your future?

Read the following excerpt from a Psalm David wrote. Think about the problem he is facing and the reason he is able to "not **despair**."

> *Teach me Your way, O LORD,*
> *And lead me in a level path*
> *Because of my foes.*
> *Do not deliver me over to the desire of my adversaries,*
> *For false witnesses have risen against me,*
> *And such as breathe out violence.*
> *I would have despaired unless I had believed that I would*
> *see the goodness of the LORD*
> *In the land of the living.*
> *Wait for the LORD;*
> *Be strong and let your heart take courage;*
> *Yes, wait for the LORD.*
> *- Psalm 27:11-14*

Do you know God well enough to trust Him as David did even when **adversaries** are out to destroy you?

Joshua
U-4, Chapters 9-12

In previous lessons, this workbook has led you through a prayer and asked you to write out your own prayer. This time, write a prayer expressing to God what you want Him to show you about His trustworthiness and how you can live reflecting that truth on a day-to-day basis.

LESSON ONE

Joshua
U-4, Lesson 1, Chapter 9

In this lesson you are going to look again at the importance of covenant and the absolute **irrevocability** of a covenant in the eyes of God. Begin this lesson by observing Joshua 9.

> Remember! God is the sovereign administrator of a **covenant**. He arbitrates when it is broken. A covenant is a solemn binding agreement.

1. As you observe the text, make sure you mark:

    a. every reference to *the land*.

    b. every occurrence of *covenant* along with synonyms terms such as *sworn* and *oath*.

    c. geographical locations.

2. Look at the map "Occupying the Land" in the Appendix. Look at where Gibeon is located. (*Hint: It is very close to Ai and Jericho.*) Circle or highlight this city so you can remember where it is as you continue to learn more about this incident.

3. Keep a close eye on Joshua – don't miss anything the text tells you about him. Jot down a few details that you learned about him as you did your observations.

4. When you finish your observations, once again list the main events of this chapter below or in the margin of your Observation Worksheet.

© 2008 Precept Ministries International

Joshua
U-4, Lesson 1, Chapter 9

5. Record the theme of Joshua 9 on the "At A Glance" chart.

6. Before you look at Joshua 10, answer the following questions.

   a. What was the Gibeonite's goal?

   b. Have you ever believed something that looked good at first, but turned out to be a lie? Write out your experience.

   c. Even though you were **deceived**, did you still suffer consequences for your poor choice? If so, what were they?

   > Do you remember the story of Eve from Genesis 3? She was deceived by the serpent and ate the fruit of the tree of life. As a result, she suffered consequences for her choice.

   d. How do you think Joshua could have avoided being deceived?

LESSON TWO

Joshua
U-4, Lesson 2, Chapter 10

1. Now, before we stop and look more closely at what you observed in Joshua 9, you need to find out what Joshua 10 has to say. Observe chapter 10.

   Don't forget to use your bookmark to mark the keywords contained in this chapter and include: *utterly destroyed* and *he left no survivor*.

2. Once again consult the map "Occupying the Land" and circle or highlight where the kings mentioned in this chapter are from and where the events recorded in this chapter occur.

3. List the flow of events covered in Joshua 10 below or on your Observation Worksheet.

4. Record the theme for Joshua 10 on the "At A Glance" chart.

© 2008 Precept Ministries International

Joshua
U-4, Lesson 2, Chapter 10

5. Finally observe where Joshua is fighting by looking at the "Occupying the Land" map in the Appendix. Is it to the north, in the central region, or the south? Where were his first **conquests**?

> This chapter has a lot of information! Have you ever wondered why God included all the details about events like these victories won by Joshua? Did you know that many people believe the Bible is just a book of fairy tales? When you look at the details of these battles and see the actual places where these events took place, do you think they could be just fairy tales? The details not only give us a clear understanding of the history of Israel, they also show Who God was in each of these battles and the kind of warrior-leader Joshua was.

LESSON THREE

Joshua
U-4, Lesson 3, Chapter 9-10

In this lesson you will take a closer look at the covenant made by the Israelites under Joshua's leadership with the Gibeonites.

> ### A CLOSER LOOK AT COVENANTS:
>
> *A covenant was a solemn binding agreement made between two parties. Sometimes the parties were individuals, families or people groups; at other times a greater person covenanted with a lesser person. In the Torah (Genesis through Deuteronomy), they were between God and man.*
>
> *God made a covenant with Abraham. It was a one-sided covenant in that God demanded nothing from Abraham. However when God made a covenant with Israel (the Law) God set conditions that Israel agreed to.*
>
> *Covenants brought parties together into a partnership that guaranteed, among other things, protection from enemies.*
>
> THE MORE YOU KNOW...

1. Think about the events of Joshua 9-10 again. Why was Israel hesitant to make a covenant with the Gibeonites (9:7)? Isn't it better to settle for peace than engage in war whatever the cost? It seems **"logical" – reasonable** – but what does God have to say about this?

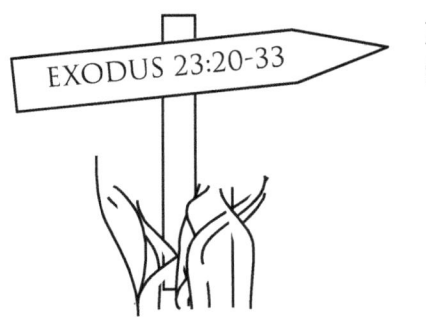

How do these verses (especially verse 32) help you understand Joshua 9:7?

© 2008 Precept Ministries International

Joshua
U-4, Lesson 3, Chapter 9-10

2. Now list everything you learn from marking the references to covenant, the oath Joshua swore to the Gibeonites. Examine each place you marked covenant in the light of the 5 Ws and an H: who, what, when, where, why and how.

3. In Joshua 9:16-27, you read of a conflict between the people and the leadership of Israel over the covenant they made with the Gibeonites.

   a. What was the conflict? Why were the people upset?

   b. What decision did the leaders make?

   c. Was it the right decision? Why or why not? *(Consider all you learned about covenant in order to answer this question.)*

LESSON FOUR

Joshua
U-4, Lesson 4, Chapters 9-10

Continue to work on understanding the significance of the events in Joshua 9 and 10 by looking at these cross-references and answering the related questions.

1. Now in light of what you observed in your previous lesson:

   a. Why do you think Israel defended the Gibeonites as recorded in Joshua 10?

   > Fill in the blanks:
   > **Cross references** – Sometimes not all the information about one person, event or topic is found in the passage you are studying; other parts of _____ give more insight or details. When you look at these other parts of _____ to understand more fully the passage you are studying, you are using Scripture to _____ Scripture.

   b. Read the verses below and mark every reference to *covenant* including the word *oath*. What do you learn from this passage about the gravity of making a covenant and not honoring it? Write it out.

2 SAMUEL 21:1-14

> By the way, the events in the book of Joshua occurred between 1405-1381 B.C. while events in 2 Samuel occurred during David's reign. David ruled from 1011 to 971 B.C.

Joshua
U-4, Lesson 4, Chapters 9-10

c. Why did David spare Jonathan's son Mephibosheth? Read the verses listed on the signpost, marking *agreement* and *oath* as you marked covenant. Write out your answer.

1 SAMUEL 20:15-17, 23, 42

2. Considering all you learned about the covenant the Israelites made with the Gibeonites – and God's sovereign administration of that covenant in David's time when Saul violated it – do you think God will ever break a covenant with you?

3. Read the following passages and write out what God promises you when you truly believe on and receive the Lord Jesus Christ – when you enter into the New Covenant.

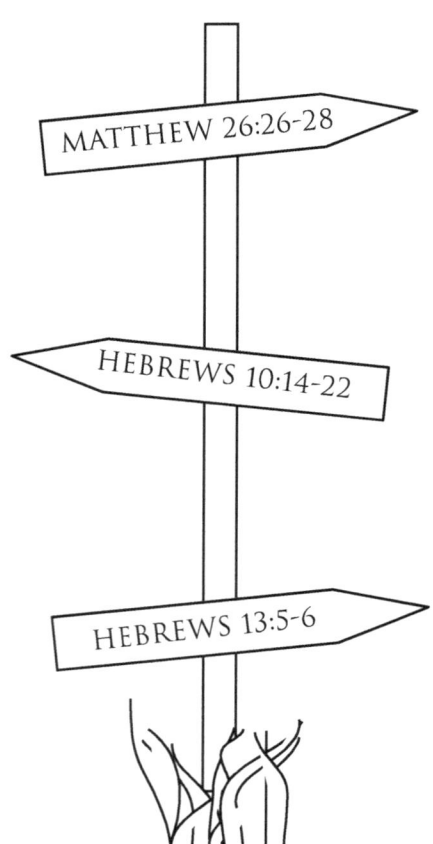

MATTHEW 26:26-28

HEBREWS 10:14-22

HEBREWS 13:5-6

96 © 2008 Precept Ministries International

Joshua
U-4, Lesson 4, Chapters 9-10

At the beginning of this unit you were asked if you found God trustworthy. From what you have seen in these four lessons, how trustworthy would you say God is? Do you see how studying how God interacted with man in the past can increase your ability to trust Him? God's Word is essential in the life of a believer!! GET INTO IT!!

Joshua
U-4, Lesson 4, Chapters 9-10

LESSON FIVE

Joshua
U-4, Lesson 5, Chapter 11

1. Observe Joshua 11. Using your key word bookmark, mark all the key words found in this chapter including:

   a. every reference to *God* (if it gives you an insight into God's character or His ways).

   b. every reference to *the land* (when it refers to the land God promised Israel).

2. After you have finished your observations note every place you double underlined a geographical location. Highlight them on the "Occupying the Land" map so you will see where these events took place.

3. Look at 11:1-5. How do these verses connect with Joshua 10? What had Jabin king of Hazor heard according to verse 1? What did he do as a result of what he knew?

That's enough for today! In the next lesson you will be working to answer some very difficult questions these chapters brought to your mind. Prayerfully ask God to give you wisdom and insight before you begin work on the next lesson.

© 2008 Precept Ministries International

Joshua
U-4, Lesson 5, Chapter 11

LESSON SIX

Joshua
U-4, Lesson 6, Chapters 10-11

In Joshua 10 and 11 you marked the key phrases *utterly destroyed* and *he left no survivor*. Why did the sons of Israel do this to the cities and inhabitants? You really need to have the answer to this question because it is something that people constantly raise up "against the knowledge of God." You may have heard things like, "Why would a loving God have His people kill every man, woman and child?" or "God isn't the scary God of the Old Testament anymore."

> "We are destroying speculations and every lofty thing raised up against the knowledge of God, and we are taking every thought captive to the obedience of Christ,"
> - 2 Corinthians 10:5

Our enemy, the devil, wants you to doubt God and question His motives. You need to know the truth to combat the lies!

1. Look up and read the text carefully and answer the following questions:

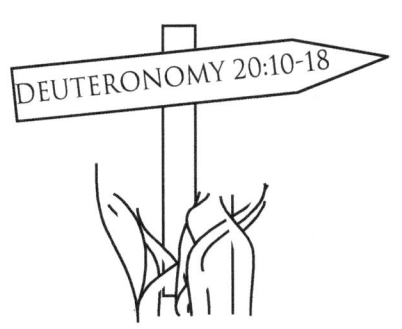

DEUTERONOMY 20:10-18

   a. Which cities are to be offered peace?

   b. What are the Israelites to do if the people do not accept the terms of peace?

   c. According to Deuteronomy 20:16-18, what are they to do to the cities within the borders of the land God has given to them?

> In Deuteronomy Moses gives the laws to the second generation of Israelites concerning how they were to live and what they were to do when they entered the Promised Land. These are the children of those who were adults when Moses led the people out of Egypt. When this first group reached the Promised Land they feared the inhabitants of the land and disobeyed God. As their consequence they were sent into the wilderness for 40 years and all the adults died there. Moses had already given the laws and commands to the first generation but now that they were all dead he gave them a second time to the new generation as they prepared to go in a take the land.

© 2008 Precept Ministries International

Joshua
U-4, Lesson 6, Chapters 10-11

d. What had the inhabitants of these cities been doing according to 20:18? Do you think this deserved punishment from God?

> **Detestable** – an adjective used to describe a disgusting thing, an abomination.

2. Look up the following passage.

GENESIS 15:12-16

a. According to verse 16, why will Abraham's descendants not possess the land until the fourth generation? *(By the way, did you recognize the group mentioned in this verse from Joshua 11:3?)*

> In Genesis 15 God makes the covenant with Abraham, the forefather of all the Israelites, guaranteeing to him and his descendents the land of the Canaanite. God tells Abraham in this passage when his descendents will possess the land and why there will be a delay. Look carefully at the passage you are reading to see the reason for the delay of ownership.
> By the way, do you know why God gets to decide whom this land belongs to? If you already studied the life of Abraham you may remember. If not, look at Genesis 14:19 and 22, to see how a priest named Melchizedek and Abraham described God.

b. What does this tell you about why God is going to take the land from the people who were living in it at the time He made the promise to Abraham?

c. What does that tell you about God? Why is He waiting?

> **Iniquity** – a noun meaning a gross injustice or wickedness; a wicked act or thing; sin.

Joshua
U-4, Lesson 6, Chapters 10-11

3. Finally, think about this question very carefully. From looking at these passages (especially Deuteronomy 20:16-18), do you think God was "unfair" or "mean" to have the sons of Israel *utterly destroy* these cities and *leave no survivor*? How would you describe to someone else why God made these commands?

You know, sometimes topics like this are confusing. They make you ask questions like, "If God is so loving, why did He have these men, women and children killed," or maybe, "I've heard of other religious groups who say they are killing people because God told them to. If He told the Israelites to do it, did He tell these people to also?" It is important for you to know God's Word and understand who He is in order to not be taken in by the many misconceptions and deceptions in the world today.

As you saw in your work today, God did not just randomly choose to destroy the people living in the land Joshua and the sons of Israel were to take. These people had committed detestable acts and God had mercifully given many years (four generations worth of time) to repent. They had not! Because God is a **just** God who cannot allow sin to go unpunished He dealt with their sin. Isn't it reassuring from that these people like Rahab were given opportunities to know who God was and respond as she did? Sadly, the majority of them chose not to turn to God. (By the way, other opportunities like these are recorded in Scripture.)

Also, it is important to understand that God did not command that these cities and people be utterly destroyed because they were not Israelites. God is the same yesterday, today, and forever. His commandments are based on His unchanging character and consistent dealing with sin. God commands believers to lovingly and compassionately share the truth about His Son with unbelievers, so they too can repent and be saved from judgment He still brings as a penalty for sin. But it is important to remember that God decides when and how to judge people and nations. He has clearly outlined in His Holy Word when that judgment will take place. (This should encourage you to continue studying so you will know the truth about these things.) Any religious group that claims God has told them something different from what His Word says is deceived and not acting as God's representatives.

You live in a very mixed up world. People are confused and deceived about who God is and what His will is for them and the world. You don't have to be confused or deceived! You have God's Word - use it! Know the truth and live by it!

Joshua
U-4, Lesson 6, Chapters 10-11

LESSON SEVEN

Joshua
U-4, Lesson 7, Chapters 10-11

In the last lesson, you looked at why God told the Israelites to *utterly destroy* the cities and inhabitants of the land. Today, you are going to look at the things God tells believers today they are to *utterly destroy*. This wasn't a command just for Joshua and the people of Israel.

1. Jabin king of Hazor sent for other kings to gather to fight Israel. What did you learn about Hazor in Joshua 10?

2. What did Joshua and the people of war do concerning Hazor?

3. Notice the note in your Bible that "utterly destroyed" can also be translated *put under the ban*. In the last unit you saw some behaviors or practices that are "under the ban" for believers. Read the verses below and answer the following questions.

   a. How should you deal with these areas of sin that are forbidden?

   b. Why is it important to put to death the sin in our lives?

© 2008 Precept Ministries International

Joshua
U-4, Lesson 7, Chapters 10-11

c. After observing how Joshua carried out the command to *utterly destroy*, how do you think you can carry out the command to "put to death" these sins? What actions or mind-set should you have in order to obey God in this area?

d. Based on what you learned about why God wanted Joshua and the people to *utterly destroy* the cities and inhabitants (Deuteronomy 20:18), why is it so important for you to put to death sin in your life?

4. Read through Joshua 10 again. This time, color key references to *God* that show God in action or that teach you about His character and/or His ways.

a. When you finish, list below what you learn about God from Joshua 10 and 11.

b. Now, do you really believe all that you have seen about God? How does such knowledge affect you? How can this be practically applied? How can it serve to make you strong and courageous – not rattled by His opponents and yours? (And there are a lot of them!!)

Joshua
U-4, Lesson 7, Chapters 10-11

 5. Record the theme of chapter 11 on the "At A Glance" chart.

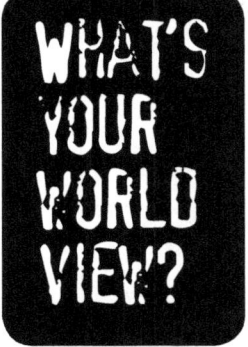

PUT TO DEATH - PROJECT

For this project you will need:

Dictionary or Word Study books *Cardboard*
Scissors *Markers*

Look up the following words from the list of things you are to put to death according to Colossians 3:5 in a dictionary or New Testament Word Study resource, and record a brief definition:

Immorality

Impurity

Passion

Evil Desire

Greed

Next, cut out a gravestone from the cardboard. Put your name at the top and then based on the definitions above, write out behaviors, thoughts and actions you need to put to death. Be specific about things you consider yourself dead to as a believer, for example: pornography, lustful thoughts, revenge, gossip, selfishness, etc.

© 2008 Precept Ministries International

Joshua
U-4, Lesson 7, Chapters 10-11

LESSON EIGHT

Joshua
U-4, Lesson 8, Chapter 12

1. Observe Joshua 12. Use your bookmark to mark all the key words contained in this chapter and be sure to include:

    a. every reference to *Moses*.

    b. every reference to *Joshua*.

2. Think through all you learned about the battle of Jericho in chapters 6-11. If you were to represent Joshua's campaign strategy by three arrows on a map, where would you place them (north, south, central) and in what order? Draw them on the map below and number them chronologically. After you have thought about this, turn to the map in the Appendix "Conquering the Land" to see if you got it right!

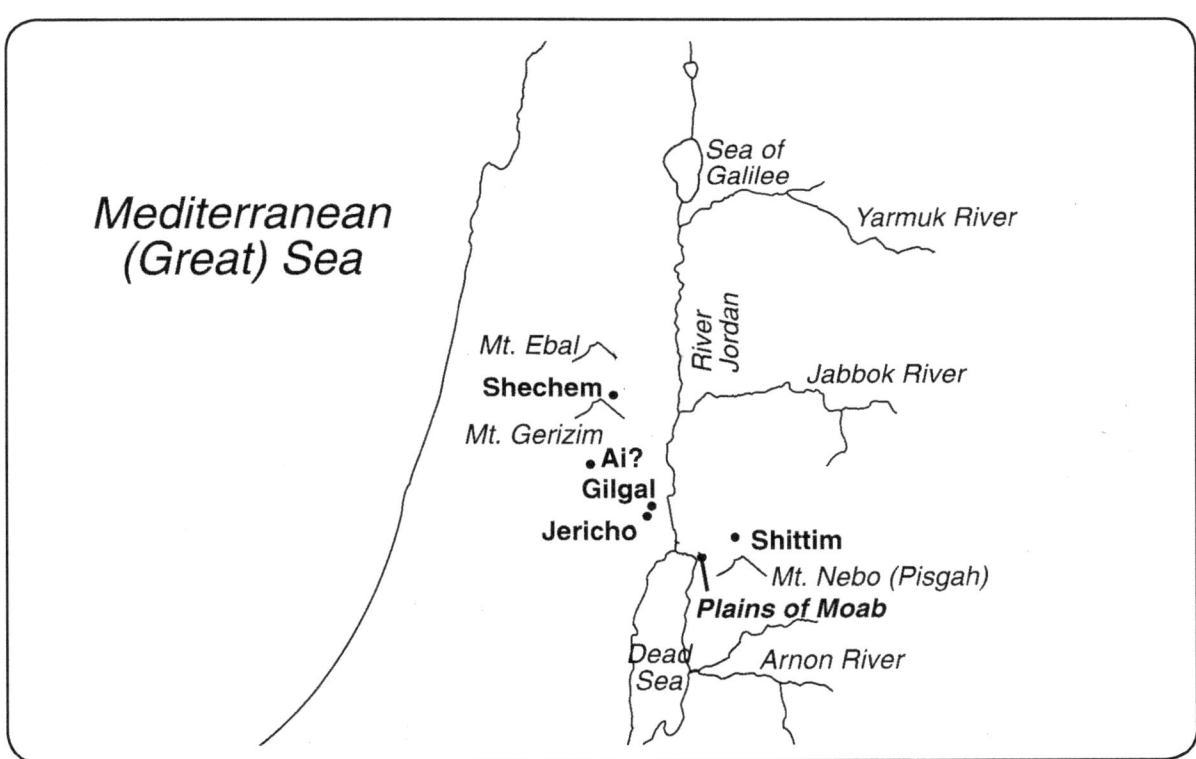

3. One last question: what is the significance of Joshua 11:16–12:24?

© 2008 Precept Ministries International

Joshua
U-4, Lesson 8, Chapter 12

a. Do you see any correlation between these verses and Joshua 1? List your insights below.

b. If you were living in Joshua's time, wouldn't you love to rehearse the great victories and conquests; to **enumerate** the blessings of God in delivering your enemies into your hands and bringing you great triumph over them?

When was the last time you sat down and listed all the blessings God has brought to your life, rehearsed all that God has done for you? It's a real faith-builder. In fact you may want to list some of your blessings, your deliverances, below. Think about what God has given you victory over during your life (a sinful habit or thought pattern, etc).

Joshua
U-4, Lesson 8, Chapter 12

 4. Record the theme of Joshua 12 on the "At A Glance" chart.

> Good job! This was a long and difficult lesson. You are doing a great job. Just like Joshua you are taking the time to learn how to become a great leader! It took time and effort for Joshua to become the warrior you are learning about. Do you want to become a leader like Joshua? Then you must start by diligently learning and growing in your knowledge and understanding of the Lord.

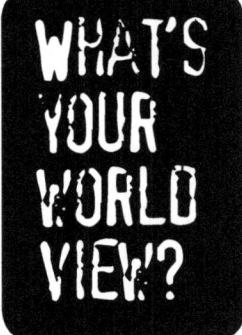

VICTORY ARTICLE – PROJECT

Imagine you are living in the days of Joshua and you are one of the warriors fighting with Joshua. Think about how encouraging it would be to hear about the many great victories God had accomplished through you. Using Joshua 11 and 12, write a letter to send to your family and friends describing these victories. As you write, think about why God had the writer of Joshua included a list of victories Israel won.

Joshua
U-4, Lesson 8, Chapter 12

Joshua
U-4, Chapters 9-12

ENRICHMENT WORDS

Adversaries – enemies that oppose, contends with or resists.

Conquest – something conquered especially territory appropriated in war.

Deceived – caused to accept as true or valid what is false or invalid, given a false impression.

Despair – to lose all hope or confidence.

Enumerate – to specify one after another; to list.

Irrevocability – not capable of being altered or changed.

Just – morally right or good.

Logical – capable of reasoning or of using reason in an orderly fashion.

Reasonable – not extreme or excessive, having a just or valid basis.

Joshua
U-4, Chapters 9-12

UNIT FIVE

Joshua
U-5 Chapters 13-17

Obedience Rewarded

Do you know where you should be or want to be with God but find that you are far from reaching that goal? Can you think of areas in your life you should change or grow in, but are choosing to remain **stagnant** because you don't want to put in the time or effort?

Today's culture is constantly bombarding you through media, movies, news, fashion, music, etc. Are the waves of culture slowly rising around you causing you to lose your firm foundation in the Word of God? If you continue to allow this ocean to overwhelm you, where will it lead?

> Is culture's noise drowning out the sound of God's Word?

Write a prayer or journal your thoughts in the space below in response to the questions above. Be honest with yourself and God.

Remember to always begin your study of God's Word in prayer. You can begin this unit by agreeing with the prayer below:

ONE ON ONE:

*O Father, speak loud and clear. Help me see what it means to possess our possessions... to live in the light of our **heritage**... to take what is ours without **compromise**.*

Speak... and may we hear, learn, and fear.

© 2008 Precept Ministries International

Joshua
U-5 Chapters 13-17

LESSON ONE

Joshua
U-5, Lesson 1, Chapter 13

1. Observe Joshua 13:1-6. Be sure to mark:

   a. any reference to the *Lord's words*.

   b. any commands given by God.

2. Compare Joshua 13:1-6 with Joshua 11:16-23. List the regions given in each passage in the appropriate column below, as well as any information given to you about the land mentioned in each passage.

JOSHUA 13:1-6	JOSHUA 11:16-23

3. Mark on the "Occupying the Land" map *at the end of this lesson* the areas mentioned in Joshua 13:1-6 in one color and the areas mentioned in 11:16-23 in another color. Then answer the following:

   a. Are these passages **contradictory**?

© 2008 Precept Ministries International

Joshua
U-5, Lesson 1, Chapter 13

    b. Why or why not?

4. Do your observations on the rest of Joshua 13, using your key word bookmark as you have been doing. Be sure to include:

    a. *inheritance*. This will become a key word from this point on in Joshua. Therefore add this to your key word bookmark. When you finish Joshua 13, go back and mark its first occurrence in Joshua 11:23.

    b. every reference to *Levi*.

    c. As you read, note which side of the Jordan is being referred to. You may want to mark whether it's the eastern side or the western side.

5. As you come to the description of each tribe's inheritance, write the name of the tribe in the margin of the text.

    6. Mark on the "Occupying the Land" map in the Appendix the land each tribe had yet to possess now that the major kings had been defeated.

7. Which tribes are dealt with first in Joshua 13? Why do you suppose God does it this way? Are they really a part of Israel?

8. List below what you learn about the tribe of Levi in this chapter.

118   © 2008 Precept Ministries International

Joshua
U-5, Lesson 1, Chapter 13

9. Look up the following cross-references. Write out what you learn about this tribe concerning the inheritance of the land and why this tribe was different from all the rest by answering the 5Ws and H questions.

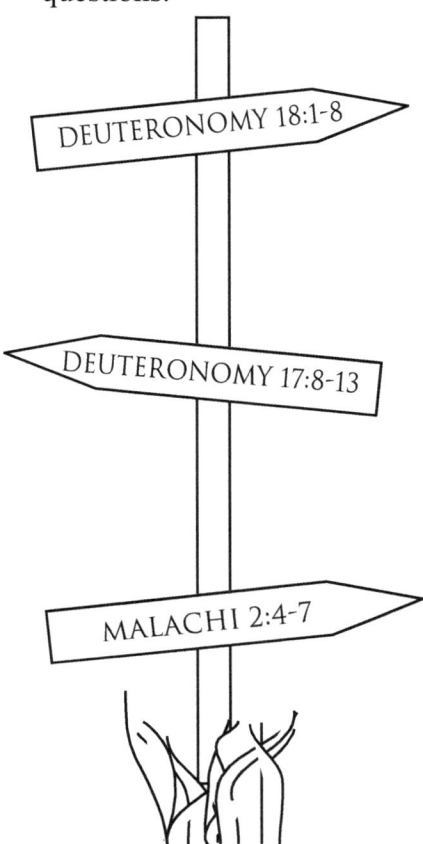

> Isn't it neat to see that the Levites did not receive any land as an inheritance because their inheritance was the Lord! The fact that God gave them the job of ministering to the people on His behalf and being in charge of ministering in the house of God was worth more than the land the other tribes got as an inheritance. Have you ever stopped to consider that serving the Lord is worth far more than any material possession? It is a blessing and an honor to serve the Lord and to serve others on His behalf.

© 2008 Precept Ministries International

Joshua
U-5, Lesson 1, Chapter 13

LESSON TWO

Joshua
U-5, Lesson 2, Chapters 13-14

1. Before you begin your work on Joshua 14, consider how God mentions various peoples that have already been defeated and destroyed in Joshua 13 – Og, Balaam, Sihon. As the people went to possess their inheritance, don't you think that when they came to the various cities – such as Beth Peor where their enemies were conquered – that those past victories, deliverances, or judgments by God would serve as an encouragement to them?

   a. How could remembering victories at these places have encouraged the people?

   b. How can you be encouraged when you are feeling overwhelmed with new tasks or responsibilities?

> **Interpretation questions** like this first question are designed for you to think about your answer. You may not always find the answer directly from the text. In order to answer these kinds of questions you need to put yourself in the place of the people in this chapter and think about the events surrounding the one you are **contemplating**. Also, because you are studying God's Word you can ask Him to help you understand.
>
> "But if any of you lacks wisdom, let him ask of God, who gives to all generously and without **reproach**, and it will be given to him."
> – James 1:5

2. Observe Joshua 14. It's a great chapter because its outstanding character is a man who followed the Lord fully. Along with the key words already listed on your bookmark, make sure to mark every reference to:

   a. *Caleb*.

   b. *following the Lord fully*.

   c. the *Lord speaking* (*the Lord spoke*).

   d. time and geographical locations. (These are important!)

Joshua
U-5, Lesson 2, Chapters 13-14

3. What happens in Joshua 14:1-5 versus the rest of the chapter?

4. Wow! Caleb is definitely someone you want to focus on in this chapter. Therefore, list everything you learn about him from Joshua 14. As you do this, keep in mind the phrases you marked in this chapter. There is a chart at the end of this lesson entitled "A Profile on Caleb" where you can list these facts.

> Caleb was an awesome man of God! Unfortunately, there are far too few examples in today's world for young people to look up to. Caleb is a tremendous example of godly manhood for young men to **emulate**. Young girls can look to Caleb to see attributes they should look for in a godly young man.

5. Now go back to Numbers 13 and 14 and see what these chapters teach us about Caleb. For those who studied the book of Numbers, this will be review; for others it will be fresh discovery. Either way you should be blessed. Mark every reference to *Caleb* and *Joshua* as you read these chapters, and then list what these chapters teach you about Caleb on the Profile chart.

6. Now, stop and think of what you learned about Caleb.

   a. What major event is Caleb remembered for in Scripture?

   b. Why was Caleb one of only two (Joshua being the other) men allowed to take possession of the land after all the other's had died in the wilderness (Numbers 14:24)?

Joshua
U-5, Lesson 2, Chapters 13-14

   c. How old is Caleb in Joshua 14, how is he described, what does he want to do, and why?

7. Now, as a student of the Word, in order to live out this truth, think about the following questions:

   a. First, what do you think it means to follow the Lord based on Caleb's example?

> Fill in the blanks:
> **Application**:
> Applying the _____
> of the text to _____ _____.

   b. What were the **benefits** for Caleb following the Lord fully, and what were the consequences for those who didn't?

> Did you realize that the choices you make today will affect your future? You know if you choose to not study you will reap the consequence of bad grades. In turn, that choice will affect which college you get into and ultimately affect what kind of job you get and in turn how you will provide for your family. But, do you also realize the choices you make concerning obedience to the Lord will affect your future far more?

   c. How can you follow the Lord fully?

   d. Now, the hard question: are you following the Lord fully? If not, what is stopping you? Write it out so you can see it in black and white.

© 2008 Precept Ministries International

Joshua
U-5, Lesson 2, Chapters 13-14

e. What long-term benefits do you think you could reap in the future for following the Lord fully? And, what consequences do you think you could face for not following the Lord fully?

f. Have you learned anything from your study of Joshua that can help you make right choices?

8. Record the themes for chapters 13 and 14 on the "At A Glance" chart.

BENEFITS AND CONSEQUENCES — PROJECT

1.
For this project you will need:

Sheet of paper   Two to three adults

Talk to two to three adults in your life and ask them to tell you of a choice they made in their past to either follow the Lord fully or not. Ask them to share with you the benefits or consequences they reaped or continue to suffer from as a result of that choice.

Then on a sheet of paper write out their story including the choice they made and either the benefit or consequences they reaped. After you record their responses write a paragraph explaining what you learned about how the choices you make today can affect your life in the future.

Write a second paragraph describing what you will do to make sure you follow the Lord fully as a result of what you learned.

LESSON THREE

Joshua
U-5, Lesson 3, Chapter 15

1. Observe Joshua 15, where you will learn more about Caleb. Mark the key words on your bookmark and be sure to include:

    a. *Caleb*. Remember if something is in the Word of God, it is there for a purpose.

    b. every reference to *driving out, dispossessing the enemy in Canaan*. (Add this to your bookmark.)

What may seem like just a lot of names and places are actually very important. As you read all these details regarding the inheritance that is being apportioned to the tribes, put yourself in their place. These people were being told after 40 years of wandering in the wilderness and then participating in many battles to drive out the inhabitants of the land that they would now get to possess it. (Don't forget this land was promised 400 years earlier to their forefather, Abraham.) What a blessing it must have been to the Israelites to have Joshua spell out the inheritance of each of the 12 tribes of Israel.

As we talk about the 12 tribes, remember the Levites received no land. Therefore, that would mean the land would have been apportioned to only eleven tribes. However, the two sons of Joseph, Manasseh and Ephraim each receive an inheritance, bringing the total to 12 tribes who take possession of the land: nine and one-half tribes west of the Jordan; and Gad, Reuben, and the half-tribe of Manasseh east of the Jordan.

Eventually God will refer to the northern kingdom of Israel (the 10 tribes that split from Judah and Benjamin after Solomon's death) as Ephraim.

2. Isn't Caleb awesome! List what you learn from Joshua 15:13-19 about Caleb on the "A Profile of Caleb" chart you started in the last lesson located at the end of the unit.

3. Now go to Judges for more insight into Caleb. Read the following passage that rehearses what happened when Caleb "took his mountain."

    a. Mark the references to *Caleb* in this passage.

    b. Record your insights on your profile sheet on Caleb.

4. From all you have learned about this amazing man, write out a one-line description of him. What do you think of when you think of Caleb?

© 2008 Precept Ministries International

Joshua
U-5, Lesson 3, Chapter 15

5. Apparently God hadn't given Caleb a son, but He gave him quite a son-in-law. Read the following passage and see what you learn about Othniel, Caleb's son-in-law. Record your insights.

 6. Record the theme of Joshua 15 on your "At A Glance" chart.

> Do you remember hearing of Caleb in stories you read or were told as a child? Do you think you understand more about him from actually looking at the biblical account for yourself? Caleb was an awesome man of God! What made him an awesome man of God? Nothing but the fact that he chose, regardless of what everyone else was doing, to follow the Lord fully. Did you notice in the Numbers account that not only did the other spies disagree with Caleb and Joshua, but all of the people sided against them as well? But that did not keep Caleb from making the right choice.
>
> When you choose to follow God you can count on others to disagree with you and maybe even turn their backs on you. When choosing whether or not to follow God fully remember the consequences that all those who chose not to follow God suffered and the great reward Caleb received for his obedience. Then you will be able to say like David, "The Lord has rewarded me according to my righteousness; According to the cleanness of my hands He has recompensed me" (Psalm 18:20). Don't forget what Proverbs 13:21 says... "Adversity pursues sinners, but the righteous will be rewarded with prosperity." Which do you want, adversity or reward?

LESSON FOUR

Joshua
U-5, Lesson 4, Chapters 16-17

1. Observe Joshua 16 and 17, marking the words from your key word bookmark and every reference to the *Canaanites*.

2. What do you learn about the daughters of Zelophehad in chapter 17?

3. In chapters 16 and 17, whose inheritance is described first – Manasseh's or Ephraim's?

4. Read the following cross-reference to see if there's a connection to the order you observed in Joshua concerning Manasseh and Ephraim.

GENESIS 48:17-20

> Remember to keep putting yourself in the shoes of the tribes that were being told about their inheritance, the land that they had waited so long for! Some of these chapters may seem long, but this is a time of great celebration and victory for all Israel. Also, know that these are important chapters to understand as you continue to study the Old Testament. Many other books talk about these locations and events. Now that you have studied them you will know what they are talking about!!!

© 2008 Precept Ministries International

Joshua
U-5, Lesson 4, Chapters 16-17

LESSON FIVE

Joshua
U-5, Lesson 5, Chapters 16-17

Since you have carefully observed Joshua 16 and 17, answer the following questions to better understand (interpret) these chapters.

1. What is the most important phrase you marked only once in Joshua 16 and only once in Joshua 17, and why?

2. What is God's promise in Joshua 13:6?

3. How does this compare to Joshua 1?

4. You were to mark every occurrence of the word *Canaanites* in Joshua 16 and 17. List what you learned from marking this word.

Joshua
U-5, Lesson 5, Chapters 16-17

5. *Canaanites* is also used two other places. Look up these references, mark them, and then record what you learn about the Canaanites from these verses.

6. Why do you think these chapters continue to emphasize the key repeated phrase *but they did not drive them [the Canaanites] out completely — yet they used them as forced labor*?

7. Were the children of Israel following what the Lord had said concerning what they were to do with the inhabitants of the land?

8. What lesson do you think God has for us today in these chapters? (Think about what you learned in prior lessons concerning the things believers are to *put to death* in their life.)

LESSON SIX

Joshua
U-5, Lesson 6, Chapters 16-17

What happens when you don't drive out enemies as God commanded? What kind of blessings do you miss out on when you do not obey God fully? That is what you are going to answer today!

1. Read the following passages and write out how they compare to what you learned in Joshua 15:63.

    a. Joshua 16:10

    b. Joshua 17:13

2. Read Joshua 17:14-18.

    a. What is the complaint of the sons of Joseph in this passage?

    b. What is their concern about the Canaanites?

    c. What is Joshua's response and what do you think about it?

> As you answer this question, think about what you have already learned concerning God's promise to the sons of Israel in chapters 1-13.
>
> Remember you never want to learn something from God's Word and then forget it. You are building, truth upon truth, **precept** upon precept to a complete or full knowledge of the Word of God!

Joshua
U-5, Lesson 6, Chapters 16-17

d. Do you see any contrast between Caleb's attitude in 14:11-12 and that of the sons of Joseph in 17:14-18? If so, what?

e. What do you do when you see "giants" and "iron chariots" (insurmountable obstacles) hindering you from accomplishing God's will? To which of these two, Caleb or the sons of Joseph, do you relate? Explain why.

> Does your focus on the obstacles keep you from experiencing victory instead of trusting God? There may be something in your life right now that looks pretty hopeless. Joseph's sons looked to the hard work it was going to take to drive out the inhabitants. They allowed the Canaanites' iron chariots to keep them from doing what God commanded them to do, even though God had promised to fight their battles for them.

LESSON SEVEN

Joshua
U-5, Lesson 7, Chapters 16-17

God's Word contains promises given to the sons of Israel to help them overcome their fears when encountering the "giants" of the land. These promises were not only to help them... they are to encourage you as well.

1. Look up the following verses and note what they say and how they would pertain to the situation in Joshua 17:14-18:

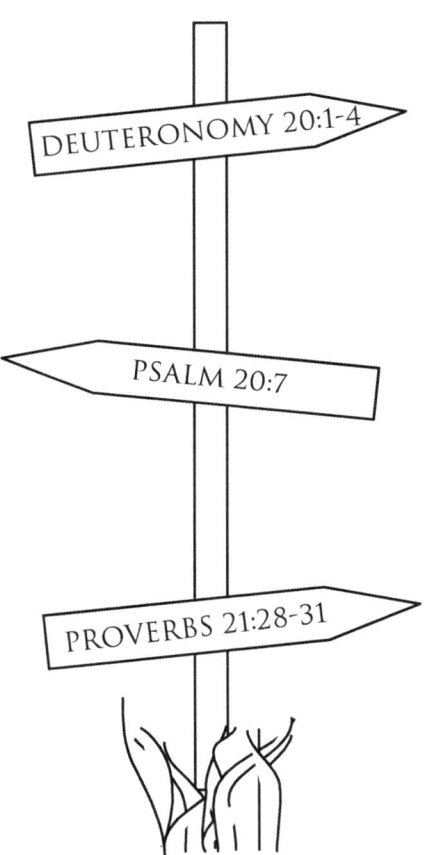

Joshua
U-5, Lesson 7, Chapters 16-17

2. According to these passages what do you need to know and remember to make sure you are not like Ephraim?

3. Record your themes for chapters 16 and 17 on the "At A Glance" chart.

4. Finally write below what you learned about God from Joshua 13-17. The goal of all Bible study is to Know God! Knowing God will result in a changed life – so what have you learned about God that has changed how you will think or live from now on?

Joshua
U-5, Lesson 7, Chapters 16-17

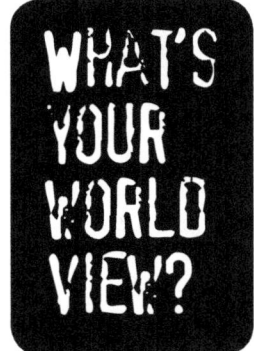

OVERCOMING GIANTS – PROJECT

For this project you will need:

Paper	*Scissors*	*Markers*
Scraps of material	*Yarn*	*Bible*

On a sheet of paper, write out some of the things you know God has called you to have victory in. For example: obeying your parents, witnessing to your friends, overcoming a sin in your life like lust, gossip, foul language, etc.

Now, using your scissors cut out two figures. Make one much bigger than the other to represent a "giant" and one smaller to represent you. Decorate these using whatever materials you want to make your giant look menacing and the smaller figure to look like you.

On the "giant," write out the obstacles that keep you from thinking you can do the things God has called you to do. For example: fear, lack of desire, ridicule, intimidation, lack of strength, etc. Then on the figure representing you, write out the promises of God you can depend on to overcome the obstacles written on the giant. If necessary, you can use your Bible to find some of the promises God has given to you. (You may also use some of the promises for the New Covenant believer you have already studied in this workbook.)

Finally, write a one paragraph summary explaining why you, as a believer, do not have to fear "giants" in your life.

Joshua
U-5, Lesson 7, Chapters 16-17

Joshua
U-5, Chapters 13-17

OCCUPYING THE LAND

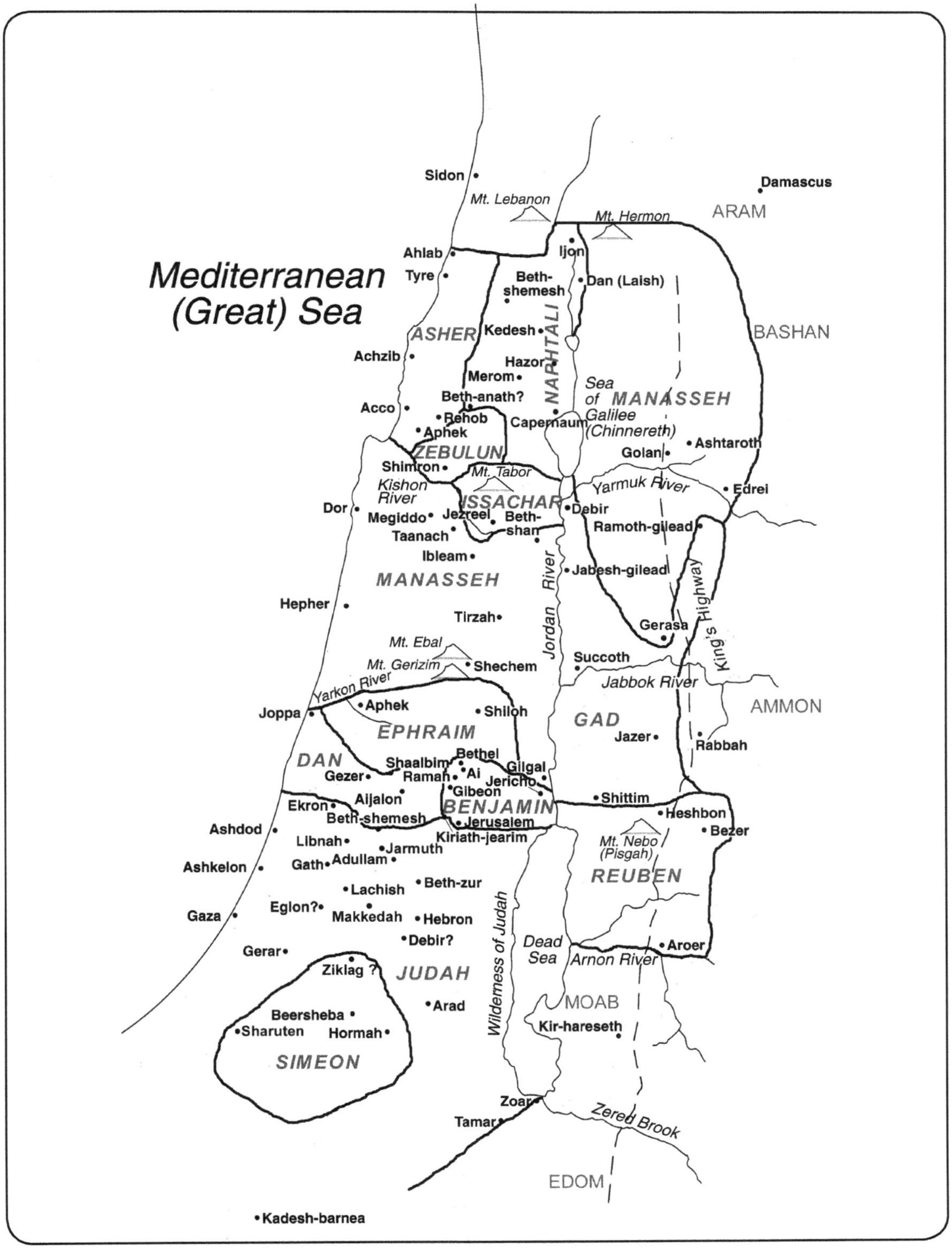

Joshua
U-5, Chapters 13-17

Joshua
U-5, Chapters 13-17

A PROFILE ON CALEB

JOSHUA 14	NUMBERS 13	NUMBERS 14

Joshua
U-5, Chapters 13-17

Joshua
U-5, Chapters 13-17

ENRICHMENT WORDS

Benefits – things that promote well-being.

Contemplating – viewing or considering with continued attention.

Contradictory – a proposition so related to another that if either of the two is true the other is false and if either is false the other must be true.

Emulate – to strive to equal or excel.

Menacing – making a show of intention to harm, representing or posing a threat to.

Precept – a command or principle intended to be a general rule of action.

Reproach – an expression of rebuke or disapproval.

Stagnant – not advancing or developing.

Joshua

UNIT SIX

Joshua
U-6, Chapters 18-21

Laziness, Murder and Responsibility

For years Joshua faithfully served under the leadership of Moses. But when Moses died, God commanded him to lead the people into the Promised Land – where enemies ruled over the land. Joshua clung to God's instructions: to be strong and courageous and follow God's Word to have victory in the land.

Now five tribes had possessed their lands, but seven still had not occupied their inheritance. What held them back? What holds you back from experiencing the riches and blessings of God's promises?

Have you evaluated your relationship with the Lord lately? Have you found yourself up against a "brick wall" of faithlessness? An unwillingness to trust God to lead you into an unchartered area of life? Perhaps you believe God is calling you to begin a relationship with someone outside your circle of friends. Maybe a new ministry opportunity has opened at your church or school.

Sometimes we just get too comfortable with our level of commitment to God and lose sight of His ongoing desire to transform our lives through His Word. Have you grown **complacent**, passive, and lazy in your pursuit of God?

> Think about these questions and then write your prayer below asking God to show you how you can continue to deepen and grow in your relationship with Him. Ask Him to renew a **zeal** for His Word and passion to grow in Christ's image.

Joshua
U-6, Chapters 18-21

LESSON ONE

Joshua
U-6, Lesson 1, Chapter 18

1. Read through Joshua 18 on your Observation Worksheets and mark the words on your key word bookmark. Also, include the following words:

   a. every reference to *Shiloh*. This is the second time Shiloh is mentioned in the Word of God; the first time is in Genesis 49:10 which falls within a prophetic blessing Jacob gave to his son Judah.

   b. *lot* or *lots*.

   > "The scepter shall not depart from Judah, nor the ruler's staff from between his feet, until Shiloh comes, and to him shall be the obedience of the peoples."
   > - Genesis 49:10

2. What are the main events in this chapter? Either list them below or in the margin of your Observation Worksheets.

3. Highlight the city of Shiloh in a distinct color on the "Occupying the Land" map in the Appendix.

   a. Where is Shiloh located in comparison to Mounts Ebal and Gerizim?

   > Notice Shiloh's central location among the tribes. The tabernacle actually remained in this city through the period of 1 Samuel, until David moved the ark to Jerusalem.

   b. If you can remember the significant event between Mounts Ebal and Gerizim that Joshua wanted his people to remember, write it out. If not, look up Joshua 8:30-35 to help you.

© 2008 Precept Ministries International

Joshua
U-6, Lesson 1, Chapter 18

4. What do you learn from Joshua 18 about Shiloh? Make sure to use the 5Ws and an H and to include the verse references.

> In the Old Testament, the lot was drawn to discover God's will for the allocation of territory (Joshua 18-19, etc.), the choice of the goat to be sacrificed on the Day of Atonement (Leviticus 16), and the detection of a guilty person (Joshua, 7:14; Jonah 1:7).

5. Why was Shiloh so important? Look at the following passage and write down what you learn about it from the text. You may want to double underline Shiloh in your Bible too!

146

© 2008 Precept Ministries International

Joshua
U-6, Lesson 1, Chapter 18

6. From what you have studied you know God told the sons of Israel that the victory was theirs. Yet according to Joshua 18, there were some tribes who would not go in and take possession of their inheritance!

   a. a. How many tribes had not taken possession of their land?

   b. What did Joshua say to these people?

   c. Do you remember the sons of Joseph's inheritance from chapters 16-17? Why hadn't they taken full possession of their land?

   d. How can the sons of Joseph and these seven tribes be examples of the complacency discussed in the introduction to this unit?

> These hesitant tribes are not unlike many believers today – they have full access to all the promises of God, yet continue to live in fear and defeat. Joshua reminds them of the victory that belongs to them. Do you even know the promises God has given you? If you do, you need to consider whether you have allowed the enemy to continue in your life (instead of putting to death the things you learned about in Colossians 3).

Joshua
U-6, Lesson 1, Chapter 18

LESSON TWO

Joshua
U-6, Lesson 2, Chapters 18-19

You're almost finished! This is the last chapter dealing with the tribes' inheritance (excluding the Levites'). While you may be tired of looking at the division of the land, remember this is the long-awaited fulfillment of God's promises to His people.

1. Observe Joshua 19 by marking the words from your key word bookmark.

2. As you come to the description of each tribe's inheritance, write the name of the tribe in the margin of the text.

3. Remember, in the original text there were no chapter or verse divisions. How are Joshua 18 and 19 connected? What event is continuing? Record it below.

4. What is the location of Joshua's inheritance?

    a. When did Joshua receive his inheritance?

    b. What can you learn about leadership from Joshua's example here?

Joshua
U-6, Lesson 2, Chapters 18-19

5. Record the themes of Joshua 18–19 on the "At A Glance" chart.

> Based on what you see in advertising, on television, in the music you listen to and from your peers, what is most important to most people? Have you noticed that everything around you is sending the message that you should be number one? That you should look out for yourself above all others? Is this the example you saw in Joshua? Absolutely not!
>
> Joshua could have had the biggest, the best, and the first pick of the land – after all he had been the mighty warrior that led God's people to the victories that got them the land in the first place. However, Joshua knew the truth – he didn't accomplish anything on his own. It was God working through him that ultimately won the victory.
>
> Joshua was more concerned with making sure the people were obedient to the Lord than with receiving his own inheritance. He knew He could trust God to reward Him as He had promised, in His timing. What kind of leaders are you following? Are they like Joshua? What kind of leader are you or will you be when God raises you up?

LESSON THREE

Joshua
U-6, Lesson 3, Chapter 20

1. Observe Joshua 20, marking the key words from your bookmark. While this is a very short chapter, it's a very important one.

2. Briefly summarize the main topic of this chapter below.

3. Who are the main characters in this chapter? Write them out below. Once you've identified these two people, mark them in a distinctive way and add them to your bookmark.

> Remember you're not just marking for the sake of coloring. You should be reading with a purpose by asking the 5Ws and H questions about the words you are marking.

> Did you know that God set up a way to deal with people who unintentionally kill others? You may be familiar with the term **manslaughter** – a legal term for someone who unintentionally kills. Although the person faces consequences, they are not as severe as those for someone who intentionally murders. Did you know that many laws your country lives by today **originated** with God?

© 2008 Precept Ministries International

151

Joshua
U-6, Lesson 3, Chapter 20

LESSON FOUR

Joshua
U-6, Lesson 4, Chapter 20

1. In the last lesson, you should have identified and marked the *avenger of blood* and the *manslayer* as the two main characters in chapter 20. If not, do it now.

    Next, fill out "The Cities of Refuge" chart at the end of the unit, listing in the appropriate columns everything you learn about the avenger of blood and the manslayer.

2. Locate on "The Cities of the Levites" map at the end of the unit the cities of refuge and highlight or mark them in a distinctive way.

3. What do you notice about where these cities are located?

Joshua
U-6, Lesson 4, Chapter 20

LESSON FIVE

1. Read the following cross references to get a better understanding of the cities of **refuge**. These passages will give you insight into what murder does to a country and the specifics of how God wants it dealt with in a society.

   This gives us valuable insights into the whole issue of the death penalty. Record what you learn on the chart you've already begun on the manslayer and the avenger of blood at the end of the unit.

2. Were these cities just for Israelites? Use the text to support your answer.

3. Life is very important to God as you can see from what you have learned about the cities of refuge. There are many additional Scriptures that deal with the **sanctity** of life. However, in the light of what you have studied:

   a. Why are these cities of refuge important?

   b. What problems might arise in a city or country if there were no system for dealing with the intentional or unintentional killing of another human being?

   c. Why are these cities spread evenly throughout the territory? Why would that be beneficial to the manslayer?

Joshua
U-6, Lesson 5, Chapter 20

    d. Why must a society deal with murder, according to Number 35:33 and Deuteronomy 19:13?

    e. Have you ever seen or experienced the consequences in a culture or society that does not deal with murder biblically? Describe what you saw or experienced.

4. Do the truths you've seen from these scriptures line up with what you believe about how murder should be dealt with? Write out your thoughts below.

> Sometimes **application** is simply choosing to believe what God says in His Word. Its not always a change of behavior.
>
> When you are confronted with the truth of God's Word you have a choice to make – Believe what God has said or not? If you choose to not believe it, then you are calling God a liar or saying His Word is inaccurate. Something to think about!

5. How do these truths compare with the laws of your state or country?

Joshua
U-6, Lesson 5, Chapter 20

RIGHT OR WRONG? – PROJECT

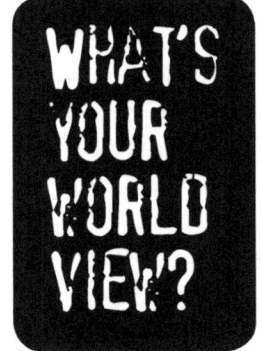

For this project you will need:

Newspapers or magazines   Internet

Find an article that describes an intentional or unintentional killing and the consequences prescribed by the judicial system. Write a half-page essay evaluating whether or not the situation was handled biblically.

Joshua
U-6, Lesson 5, Chapter 20

LESSON SIX

Joshua
U-6, Lesson 6, Chapter 21

Today we will study Joshua 21 – only three chapters remain in the book. There are few adult believers who will study God's Word this in-depth, let alone many young men or women. Such accomplishments, unfortunately, are becoming more and more rare among those who profess to know Jesus Christ and to be members of His Church. In fact, you may realize you're in the **minority** of your generation. You are to be commended for your diligence. As Paul said to Timothy, "Don't let anyone look down on you because you are young, but be an example…." You are an example when you study and apply truths that you are learning.

1. Observe Joshua 21 and mark the words from your key word bookmark.

2. Now go back and color-code the families of the Levites:

    - Sons of Kohath—Kohathites
    - Sons of Gershon—Gershonites
    - Sons of Merari—Merarites
    - Sons of Aaron

    As you come to the description of each family's inheritance, write the name of the family in the margin of the text. Also, record the number of cities allotted to each one.

A CLOSER LOOK AT LEVI:

Below is a family tree showing part of the line of Levi taken from Exodus 6.

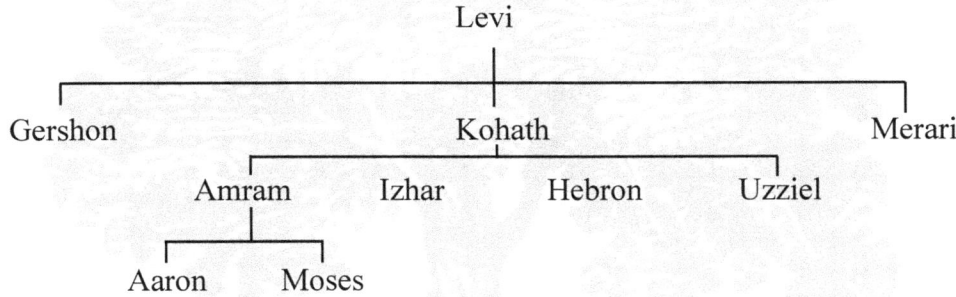

In Exodus 28 the Lord told Moses to make holy garments for Aaron and his sons and anoint them as priests to Him. Only those of the line of Aaron would be priests. The rest of the family of Kohathites and all the sons of Gershon and Merari would be Levites who would serve the priests (Numbers 3:6; 8:19).

THE MORE YOU KNOW!...

Joshua
U-6, Lesson 6, Chapter 21

3. What do the Levites speak about to Joshua?

4. What is the solution?

5. As you observe each segment of the chapter, you will see what each tribe is giving to the specific families.

    a. Locate these cities on the map, "The Cities of the Levites."

   b. Color each city according to the code you have given each of the families of the Levites.

LESSON SEVEN

Joshua
U-6, Lesson 7, Chapter 21

1. Review your observations from Unit Five, Lesson One, number nine and write down what you observed in respect to the duties of the Levites.

2. Carefully look at your map of the "Cities of the Levites." What do you notice about how these cities were distributed throughout the land?

3. If the Levites did what they were supposed to do, how would this impact the life, culture, and beliefs of the people in their cities and the cities around them?

   a. Believers today have Jesus Christ—the faithful High Priest. If Jesus is the High Priest, who are the other priests on earth today according to this verse?

   b. What is the believers responsibility according to 1 Peter?

© 2008 Precept Ministries International

Joshua
U-6, Lesson 7, Chapter 21

4. If every believer is a priest, what does that say about a believer's role within the cities and communities God has placed them in? What parallels do you see between the Levites' responsibilities and the believer's today?

5. Is your church, youth group, or school **impacting** the community by sharing and teaching God's Word and living exemplary lives? How?

6. If it's not, then what are you personally going to begin doing now that you know what you are and what your responsibility is?

7. Record themes for Joshua 20 and 21 on the "At A Glance" chart.

Joshua
U-6, Lesson 7, Chapter 21

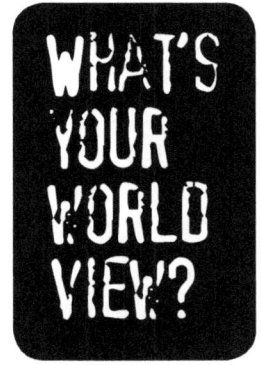

IMPACTING THE COMMUNITY – PROJECT

Find out what ministry opportunities your church, school or local ministry has for reaching the community. Select one of the ministries that most interest you and then interview one of its leaders. Write a half-page essay explaining how it is effectively sharing the Word with nonbelievers and what its impact has been locally. Then prayerfully consider whether or not God is calling you to come alongside them!

Joshua
U-6, Lesson 7, Chapter 21

LESSON EIGHT

Joshua
U-6, Lesson 8, Chapter 21

1. Read Joshua 21:43-45 again – slowly and aloud. Absorb the truths of these verses and **meditate** on them. In the light of all that you have studied these past six weeks, how significant do you think these verses are and why?

2. Make a list of everything the Lord had done for Israel according to these verses.

3. Now think about all that you have studied concerning the taking of the land. Were there defeats, rebellions, times of fear and discouragement? Briefly list some examples.

4. Did these situations prevent God from fulfilling His promises? How do you know?

© 2008 Precept Ministries International

Joshua
U-6, Lesson 8, Chapter 21

5. How does all this apply to you? Have you ever thought God would give up on you because of your failures and faithlessness? What do you know now that can help you when thoughts like this torment you again? Write it out.

6. Finally, read the following passages and answer the questions below.

a. What do these passages guarantee a believer?

b. The word *knowledge* is a key repeated word in 2 Peter. Why is studying and living out God's Word so important?

c. Do you see any parallels between Joshua and these passages? List them below.

Did you realize when you began this week's unit that you would walk away with such amazing, life-changing truths? When God asked Joshua to record the history of Israel's possession of the land, He did it to show us how He dealt with His people and His faithfulness in carrying out His Word. Aren't you thankful to know that not one of God's promises failed? You might take a few minutes to consider all you've studied and write out a prayer or journal entry about what you want to say to Him, what you want to thank Him for, and what commitments you want to make. Just don't make them lightly!

Joshua
U-6, Chapters 18-21

THE CITIES OF REFUGE CHART

THE MANSLAYER	THE AVENGER OF BLOOD
 Where?	 How?
 Who?	 When?
 Why?	 What?

Joshua
U-6, Chapters 18-21

Joshua
U-6, Chapters 18-21

THE CITIES OF THE LEVITES

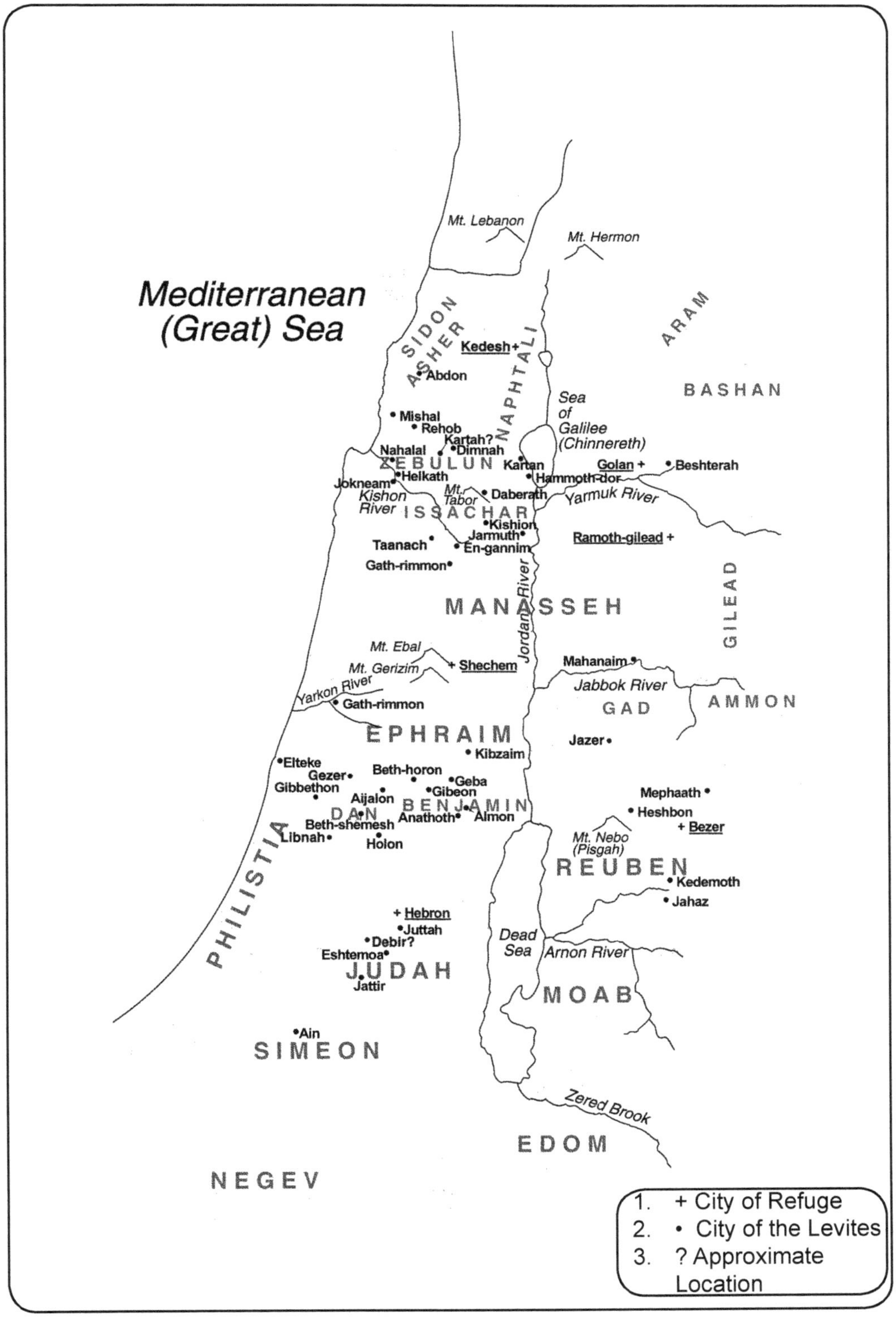

Joshua
U-6, Chapters 18-21

Joshua
U-6, Chapters 18-21

ENRICHMENT WORDS

Complacent – self-satisfied, even when accompanied by unawareness of actual dangers or deficiencies.

Dispersed - to cause to become spread widely, to spread or distribute from a fixed or constant source.

Impacting – having a direct effect or impact on.

Manslaughter – unlawful killing of a human being without express or implied malice.

Meditate – focus one's thoughts on; reflect, ponder.

Minority – a group less than half of a population differing from the majority in some characteristics.

Originated – the point at which something started, began, rose or from which it was derived.

Refuge – shelter or protection from danger or distress.

Sanctity – the quality or state of being holy or sacred.

Zeal – eagerness and ardent interest in pursuit of something.

Joshua
U-6, Chapters 18-21

UNIT SEVEN

The Battle Ends

Joshua
U-7, Chapters 22-24

Listen, O my people, to my instruction;
Incline *your ears to the words of my mouth.*
I will open my mouth in a **parable**;
I will utter dark sayings of old,
Which we have heard and known,
And our fathers have told us.
We will not conceal them from their children,
But tell to the generation to come the praises of the LORD,
And His strength and His wondrous works that He has done.

For He established a testimony in Jacob,
And appointed a law in Israel,
Which He commanded our fathers,
That they should teach them to their children,
That the generation to come might know, even the
  children yet to be born,
That they may arise and tell them to their children,
That they should put their confidence in God
And not forget the works of God,
But keep His commandments.
  - Psalm 78:1-7

ONE ON ONE: PRAYER

O Father, as we look at the farewells in these last three chapters of Joshua and as we say farewell to our study of Joshua, may the truths we have stored in our hearts be brought to our remembrance, even as the memorials that were set up in Joshua's time reminded Your **elect** *nation of Your faithfulness. May we look at the cost and choose to serve You all the days of our lives—to be strong and courageous, not dismayed by the faces of the godless. May we be obedient, valiant warriors of our Savior who fought for us, won the victory, and conquered sin and death. How we look forward to the day when we shall rule with Him.*

Now bring us to our knees as we complete our study of this awesome book You preserved for us. May we choose to serve You and You only, this day and every day so that many in our generation will see the abundant life You give. After us, may the next generation choose and serve You because we have served and honored You in strength and courage.

Joshua
U-7, Chapters 22-24

Write a prayer asking God to show you the importance of these last few chapters in the book of Joshua or a journal entry with your thoughts and expectations as you complete your journey through this book.

LESSON ONE

Joshua
U-7, Lesson 1, Chapter 22

1. Before you read Joshua 22, you need to understand the context. Read the following passage and list who Moses is talking to and the promises he and the people make.

> Remember cross-references provide additional insight on text you are studying by giving additional context. This is called consulting the whole counsel of God.

2. Chapter 22 is a very important chapter with key precepts for your life, so observe it well. As you mark key words that appear on your bookmark, also mark the following:

   a. *altar.*
   b. *witness.*
   c. *unfaithful act, act unfaithfully.*
   d. *turn away from following the Lord.*
   e. *tabernacle.*
   f. *rest.*

> **Marking Words** - When you have a long list of words to mark, it's important to remember that slowing down is key to good observation. Only mark two or three words at one time. Then go back, re-read the chapter, and mark the additional words. By the time you're finished, you'll discover you've begun memorizing the scriptures!

> This is a long chapter, student of the Word, so this is all you will look at today. You will take a closer look in the next lesson.

© 2008 Precept Ministries International

Joshua
U-7, Lesson 1, Chapter 22

LESSON TWO

Joshua
U-7, Lesson 2, Chapter 22

1. List the main events of chapter 22 either in the space below or in the margins of your Observation Worksheets.

2. How were the promises the Reubenites, Gaddites, and half-tribe of Manasseh made to Moses fulfilled?

Joshua
U-7, Lesson 2, Chapter 22

3. What major problem occurred in Joshua 22?

4. Since this is the main event in this chapter, read through Joshua 22 again and record below the problem that the nine-and-a-half tribes west of the Jordan have with the two-and-a-half tribes that built an altar after they crossed the Jordan. Why were they so upset?

   Then in the other column, record what you learn about the Reubenites, Gaddites, and the half-tribe of Manasseh's plans for that altar. Make sure you list what each side was going to do and why.

THOSE WEST OF THE JORDAN	THOSE EAST WHO BUILD AN ALTAR
What?	What?
Why?	Why?

5. Stop now and think about what each group thought and what they intended to do about it. Was either side wrong in the action it wanted to take if its understanding was correct?

Joshua
U-7, Lesson 2, Chapter 22

6. Read the following passage for additional understanding concerning why those west of the Jordan took the action they did. Write down what you learn.

> While there clearly was a misunderstanding between the tribes of Israel on either side of the Jordan, isn't it exciting to see their zeal for the Lord – the desire to serve God completely just as Joshua had commanded them? When God made you His child – brought you out of the domain of darkness into His kingdom – do you remember the overwhelming desire you had to serve Him? How are you doing today? Do you still feel compelled to do His work, to please Him in all you say and do? Do you think about your choices of friends, clothes, priorities, etc. and line them up with the Word of God? If not, ask God to renew your love and passion to do His will.

© 2008 Precept Ministries International

Joshua
U-7, Lesson 2, Chapter 22

LESSON THREE

Joshua
U-7, Lesson 3, Chapter 22

1. Look at the passage below and answer the following questions.

   a. What is the problem in the Corinthian church?

   b. How had they dealt with it?

   c. How did the Corinthians' response differ from the response of the sons of Israel in Joshua 22?

   d. Have you ever ignored the sin in one of your Christian friend's lives? If so, why?

   e. How should you respond when hearing of a fellow believer engaging in sin based on what you have learned from these two examples?

Joshua
U-7, Lesson 3, Chapter 22

2. The tribes on both sides of the Jordan had a desire to please God and not allow sin to **infiltrate** their land. Does this speak to you in any way? If so, how?

3. Finally, read Joshua 22:5 and turn it into a personal prayer. You might want to write it out.

LESSON FOUR

Joshua
U-7, Lesson 4, Chapter 23

Before we continue, take this opportunity to think of all the things God has taught you about Joshua. You have watched as he was attending Moses, victorious over Amalek, spying out the land, assuming the leadership of the nation, crossing the Jordan with strength and courage, learning to be dependent on God at Jericho and Ai, leading strategic battles from Shiloh! You have seen what God does with a life intent on knowing God through His Word – a successful and prosperous life.

Joshua is now old. He has led God's people throughout his life, but he wants now to make sure they continue to follow the Lord fully after his death. His voice echoes throughout time to hearts today. Listen closely as the Lord uses his words to speak to your heart!

1. Observe Joshua 23. Mark the key words on your list, including any of those you marked in Lesson One. Also mark every reference to the *nations* – a key word in this chapter.

2. On the chart at the end of this lesson, "Joshua's Words in Chapter 23," list what you learn about: Joshua, the leaders of Israel, the nations, and God.

3. Read the following passage and compare your observations with what you've just read in Joshua 23.

Joshua
U-7, Lesson 4, Chapter 23

4. Describe what Joshua is doing in chapter 23.

   a. Who does Joshua credit for the great victories in the land?

   b. What does this teach you about the victories in your life? Who do you give the credit?

   > Every good thing bestowed and every perfect gift is from above, coming down from the Father of Lights with whom there is not variation, or shifting shadow.
   > —James 1:17

   c. Compare what Joshua says to what God told Joshua in chapter one.

   d. What warnings does Joshua give? List specific things the sons of Israel are to avoid (*put under the ban*).

   e. What are the consequences of not following Joshua's commands?

Joshua
U-7, Lesson 4, Chapter 23

5. List the main events either in the space provided below or in the margin of your Observation Worksheet.

> This step in inductive study helps you remember the main events of the chapter. When you have completed this study you may want to transfer your notes to your Bible. Then, when you look back at this book in the Bible you can remember the things that God has personally taught you because you can quickly remember what you studied! When your pastor or youth pastor teaches on this topic, you will be right there with him because of your diligence.

> Joshua is reminding the people of God about their God – His victories and their responsibility to trust Him to drive out their enemies. Joshua is living proof to these men that success and prosperity come through meditating on God's Word day and night, and being careful to do it. This was the message that God gave Moses, Moses gave to Joshua, and God gave to Joshua when he became the leader of Israel. The message is the same for you today – know the Word!
>
> Yet, Joshua also cautions the people. He uses very **vivid** language to describe what happens if this Word is not kept, if the people begin to cling to the nations instead of clinging to their God. How vital for you to listen to Joshua's caution!
>
> Are you associating with the enemy? Analyze your life and think about the subtle ways you have adopted our culture's thinking, attitudes, and behaviors. Sometimes you have to consciously evaluate what you're doing and saying because it can be so easy to get caught up in the world. Being still before God, recounting His great works in your life, and basking in His holy light can reveal dark areas that have crept in.

© 2008 Precept Ministries International

Joshua
U-7, Lesson 4, Chapter 23

LESSON FIVE

Joshua
U-7, Lesson 5, Chapter 23

1. Read this passage and answer the following questions:

   a. Do you see parallels between this and Joshua's instructions to the Israelites in Joshua 23:12?

   b. Based on the definition of "bound" in the word study scroll and what you read in 2 Corinthians, what are believers today forbidden to do?

   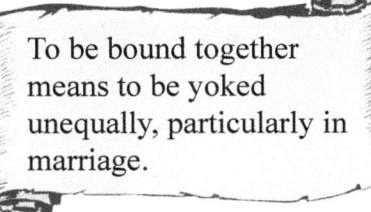

   To be bound together means to be yoked unequally, particularly in marriage.

2. Now read this verse and answer the following questions.

   a. Do you see any parallels between this verse and Joshua 23:7?

   b. What "gods" does the world serve or bow down to today? How do they serve people?

   c. How would a believer "associate" or "make friends" with the world by serving the "gods" you listed above?

Joshua
U-7, Lesson 5, Chapter 23

3. Now read this verse and answer the following:

   a. How can a believer keep from serving the "gods" of this world?

   b. What day-to-day pressures are you facing that make it difficult not to conform to the world?

4. Read this final verse and answer the following questions:

   a. How can believers renew their minds according to these verses?

   "Reprove" means to point out what is wrong. "Correct" means to make wrong right, to make crooked straight.

   b. What then should you be doing to make sure you are not friends with the world, conforming to its way of life?

Joshua
U-7, Lesson 5, Chapter 23

5. You may be asking, "How can I interact with unbelievers if I am serving the one true God?" Read the following verses and note what you learn from each. Then answer the related questions.

   a. According to these verses, is the believer supposed to ignore or "stay away" from unbelievers?

   b. What is the responsibility of the believer?

   c. How would you explain to someone else how the believer is to accomplish this responsibility without becoming friends with or conforming to the world?

© 2008 Precept Ministries International

Joshua
U-7, Lesson 5, Chapter 23

6. What comparison do you see in Joshua 23:14-16? When you find it, make a note in the margin of your Observation Worksheet.

> **Comparisons** refer to things that are similar or alike. Words such as "like" or "just as" signify a comparison.

7. What does this teach you about the character of God?

8. What application can you make to your life from this comparison? Do you hold fast to God's promises of blessing but ignore His warnings thinking, "Surely God wouldn't…?"

FRIEND OR ENEMY – PROJECT

1.
2. Think about what you learned in James 4:4 – that friendship with the world is hostility toward God. Some Christians have become "friends" with the world in the way that they dress, act, talk and alter the meaning of the Word of God to become more "tolerant." Write a brief essay describing a celebrity or other public figure who professes to be a believer but whose behavior opposes what you know to be true in the Bible.

Joshua
U-7, Lesson 5, Chapter 23

There is a lot to think about in chapter 23, isn't there? Things we need to meditate on. The Word of God is still relevant to where you are, right now, today. God knows the enemy! He knows the **ploys** and devices the enemy uses to try to deceive you. Right now you are doing the very thing Joshua spoke of so long ago—"Be very firm, then, to keep and do all that is written in the book of the law of Moses, so that you may not turn aside from it to the right hand or to the left...." Live out what you are learning.

Joshua
U-7, Lesson 5, Chapter 23

LESSON SIX

Joshua
U-7, Lesson 6, Chapter 24

Well, you have come to the final chapter in the book of Joshua. Can you believe how quickly this time passed and how much you learned about your God, His chosen nation, and your walk with Him?

1. Observe Joshua 24 and examine it in the light of the 5 Ws and an H. See where the people are, who is speaking, and to whom. Mark the key words from your bookmark, including *serve*.

2. Once again (and for the last time) list the main events of this chapter in the space provided or in the margin of your Observation Worksheet.

3. One prominent key word in this chapter is *serve*.

   a. What do you learn from marking *serve*?

   b. What options does Joshua give those who refuse to serve God?

Joshua
U-7, Lesson 6, Chapter 24

    c. And what about you? If you are not going to serve God, whom or what will you serve? (It will be someone or something.)

    d. Do you think the consequences of your actions will be any different from those of the sons of Israel? Why or why not?

4. You have seen Joshua calling the sons of Israel to serve the Lord in this chapter. Read Joshua 24:19. What is he talking about when he says that God will not forgive their transgressions or their sins? Read the passage below for further help in answering this question.

DEUTERONOMY 29:14-21

5. Record the themes of Joshua 22, 23, and 24 on the "At A Glance" chart.

LESSON SEVEN

Joshua
U-7, Lesson 6, Chapter 24

1. Read through Joshua 24 again.

2. It's interesting that the tabernacle is in Shiloh, but Joshua gathers the people to Shechem. What is significant about this place?

   Let's trace the different events that occurred in Shechem and see what we can learn. Look up the following cross-references, check their context, and then record what happened there.

   Context – The environment or setting in which something dwells or is found; what is in front or behind.

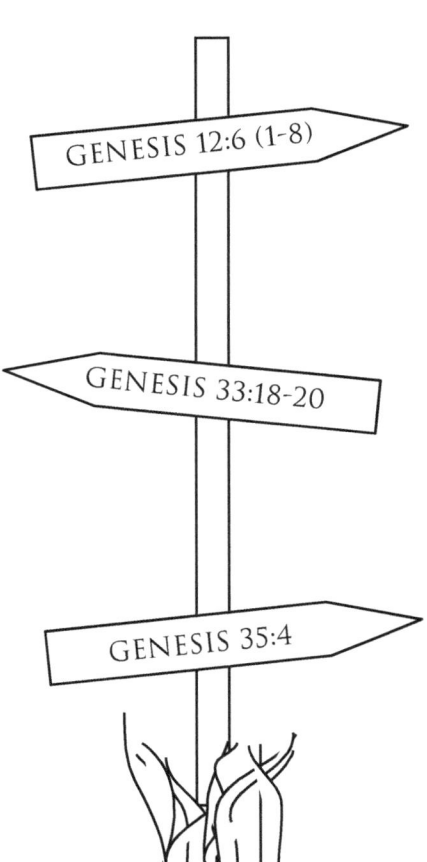

© 2008 Precept Ministries International

195

Joshua
U-7, Lesson 6, Chapter 24

3. Now, can you see any correlation between what happened in Shechem previously with what is occurring in Joshua 24? Explain.

> Joshua brings to a close the more than 400-year journey from promise to fulfillment for the children of Israel at the very site where the promise was first established. Can you imagine? How much excitement and sense of accomplishment the people must have felt. Have you ever seen God's promise from beginning to fulfillment in your life? How did it feel to remember the promise God had given you and then to stand in **awe** as you looked back at the journey? If you haven't ever experienced this, in the next lesson you will walk through this process through the story of Joseph's bones.

LESSON EIGHT

PRECEPT UPON PRECEPT®

Joshua
U-7, Lesson 7, Chapter 24

1. Read the chapter below, the last chapter in the book of Deuteronomy, and compare it with Joshua 24.

2. Now, note the relationship between Joshua 24:32 and the following verses.

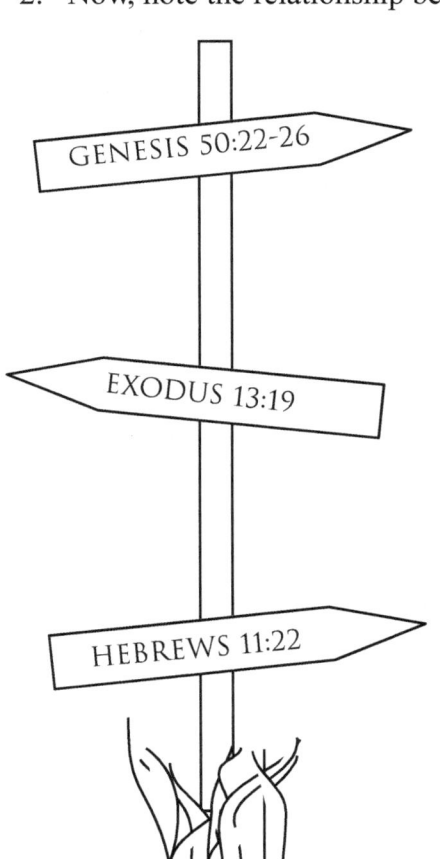

a. What did Joseph believe about God?

b. How do you know according to the verse in Hebrews that Joseph really believed this?

c. What does the burial of Joseph's bones (Joshua 24:32) prove?

© 2008 Precept Ministries International

Joshua
U-7, Lesson 7, Chapter 24

3. What does Joshua want the children of Israel to remember?

4. How does this fulfillment of God's promises speak to you? What will God do in your life?

5. In many past lessons, we have looked at what we learned about God. Take this opportunity to look over what you learned about God in chapters 22-24 by looking through your Observation Worksheets. This should be a time of worship – responding to truths you learned about Him. Record new things you see about God below.

> Now you can see one of the purposes of marking – it allows you to easily do a topical study on God's sovereignty in the book of Joshua with just a glance!

Joshua
U-7, Lesson 7, Chapter 24

6. Read the following passage and note what you learn about what God promised Israel in these verses.

7. How does this relate to Joshua 24:13?

8. You have finished listing the themes of Joshua on the "Joshua At A Glance" chart; now complete the chart.

Study the content of the chapters and look at how chapters can be grouped together in light of the content of the book. Record these under "Segment Divisions."

> **Segment Divisions** are a major division in a book, such as a group of verses or chapters that deal with the same subject, person, place or event.
>
> If you have an Inductive Study Bible (either the IISB or the new smaller NISB), you can transfer this information to the "Joshua At A Glance" chart at the end of the book of Joshua.

Joshua
U-7, Lesson 7, Chapter 24

You have completed your study on Joshua, but as you have seen, God's work in your life is never finished. He is faithful to carry out His purposes for you. You have been **equipped** with the Word of God to be a warrior-leader like Joshua. You too can know success and the first-hand power of God if you walk according to His ways.

You have finished a great course, but remember, just as God was faithful to bless those who walked according to the truth, He will hold you **accountable** for all that you know. Don't allow these powerful lessons to become a faint memory... meditate on them, be **transformed** by them and use them for God's kingdom. Become a warrior-leader like Joshua!!

Joshua
U-7, Chapters 22-24

ENRICHMENT WORDS

Accountable - subject to giving a statement explaining one's conduct.

Awe - an emotion variously combining dread, veneration, and wonder that is inspired by authority or by the sacred or sublime.

Elect - chosen for salvation by grace.

Equipped - to furnish for service or action by appropriate provisioning.

Incline - to lean, tend, or become drawn toward an opinion or course of conduct.

Infiltrate - to enter or become established in gradually, or unobtrusively usually for subversive purposes.

Parable - a usually short fictitious story that illustrates a moral attitude or religious principle.

Ploys - a tactic intended to embarrass or frustrate an opponent.

Transformed - to change in character or condition.

Vivid - strong or clear impression on the senses.

Joshua

APPENDIX

Joshua

CONTENTS:

- JOSHUA OBSERVATION WORKSHEETS

- JOSHUA AT A GLANCE CHART

- OCCUPYING THE LAND MAP

- CONQUERING THE LAND MAP

- ABOUT PRECEPT MINISTRIES INTERNATIONAL

Joshua

Joshua
Chapter 1

JOSHUA 1
OBSERVATION WORKSHEET

Chapter Theme _____

NOW it came about after the death of Moses the servant of the LORD, that the LORD spoke to Joshua the son of Nun, Moses' servant, saying,

2 "Moses My servant is dead; now therefore arise, cross this Jordan, you and all this people, to the land which I am giving to them, to the sons of Israel.

3 "Every place on which the sole of your foot treads, I have given it to you, just as I spoke to Moses.

4 "From the wilderness and this Lebanon, even as far as the great river, the river Euphrates, all the land of the Hittites, and as far as the Great Sea toward the setting of the sun will be your territory.

5 "No man will be able to stand before you all the days of your life. Just as I have been with Moses, I will be with you; I will not fail you or forsake you.

6 "Be strong and courageous, for you shall give this people possession of the land which I swore to their fathers to give them.

7 "Only be strong and very courageous; be careful to do according to all the law which Moses My servant commanded you; do not turn from it to the right or to the left, so that you may have success wherever you go.

8 "This book of the law shall not depart from your mouth, but you shall meditate on it day and night, so that you may be careful to do according to all that is written in it; for then you will make your way prosperous, and then you will have success.

9 "Have I not commanded you? Be strong and courageous! Do not tremble or be dismayed, for the LORD your God is with you wherever you go."

10 Then Joshua commanded the officers of the people, saying,

11 "Pass through the midst of the camp and command the people, saying, 'Prepare provisions for yourselves, for within three days you are to cross this Jordan, to go in to possess the land which the LORD your God is giving you, to possess it.'"

12 To the Reubenites and to the Gadites and to the half-tribe of Manasseh, Joshua said,

© 2008 Precept Ministries International

Joshua
Chapter 1

13 "Remember the word which Moses the servant of the LORD commanded you, saying, 'The LORD your God gives you rest and will give you this land.'

14 "Your wives, your little ones, and your cattle shall remain in the land which Moses gave you beyond the Jordan, but you shall cross before your brothers in battle array, all your valiant warriors, and shall help them,

15 until the LORD gives your brothers rest, as He gives you, and they also possess the land which the LORD your God is giving them. Then you shall return to your own land, and possess that which Moses the servant of the LORD gave you beyond the Jordan toward the sunrise."

16 They answered Joshua, saying, "All that you have commanded us we will do, and wherever you send us we will go.

17 "Just as we obeyed Moses in all things, so we will obey you; only may the LORD your God be with you as He was with Moses.

18 "Anyone who rebels against your command and does not obey your words in all that you command him, shall be put to death; only be strong and courageous."

Joshua
Chapter 2

JOSHUA 2
OBSERVATION WORKSHEET

Chapter Theme _____

THEN Joshua the son of Nun sent two men as spies secretly from Shittim, saying, "Go, view the land, especially Jericho." So they went and came into the house of a harlot whose name was Rahab, and lodged there.

2 It was told the king of Jericho, saying, "Behold, men from the sons of Israel have come here tonight to search out the land."

3 And the king of Jericho sent word to Rahab, saying, "Bring out the men who have come to you, who have entered your house, for they have come to search out all the land."

4 But the woman had taken the two men and hidden them, and she said, "Yes, the men came to me, but I did not know where they were from.

5 "It came about when it was time to shut the gate at dark, that the men went out; I do not know where the men went. Pursue them quickly, for you will overtake them."

6 But she had brought them up to the roof and hidden them in the stalks of flax which she had laid in order on the roof.

7 So the men pursued them on the road to the Jordan to the fords; and as soon as those who were pursuing them had gone out, they shut the gate.

8 Now before they lay down, she came up to them on the roof,

9 and said to the men, "I know that the LORD has given you the land, and that the terror of you has fallen on us, and that all the inhabitants of the land have melted away before you.

10 "For we have heard how the LORD dried up the water of the Red Sea before you when you came out of Egypt, and what you did to the two kings of the Amorites who were beyond the Jordan, to Sihon and Og, whom you utterly destroyed.

11 "When we heard it, our hearts melted and no courage remained in any man any longer because of you; for the LORD your God, He is God in heaven above and

Joshua
Chapter 2

on earth beneath.

12 "Now therefore, please swear to me by the LORD, since I have dealt kindly with you, that you also will deal kindly with my father's household, and give me a pledge of truth,

13 and spare my father and my mother and my brothers and my sisters, with all who belong to them, and deliver our lives from death."

14 So the men said to her, "Our life for yours if you do not tell this business of ours; and it shall come about when the LORD gives us the land that we will deal kindly and faithfully with you."

15 Then she let them down by a rope through the window, for her house was on the city wall, so that she was living on the wall.

16 She said to them, "Go to the hill country, so that the pursuers will not happen upon you, and hide yourselves there for three days until the pursuers return. Then afterward you may go on your way."

17 The men said to her, "We shall be free from this oath to you which you have made us swear,

18 unless, when we come into the land, you tie this cord of scarlet thread in the window through which you let us down, and gather to yourself into the house your father and your mother and your brothers and all your father's household.

19 "It shall come about that anyone who goes out of the doors of your house into the street, his blood shall be on his own head, and we shall be free; but anyone who is with you in the house, his blood shall be on our head if a hand is laid on him.

20 "But if you tell this business of ours, then we shall be free from the oath which you have made us swear."

21 She said, "According to your words, so be it." So she sent them away, and they departed; and she tied the scarlet cord in the window.

22 They departed and came to the hill country, and remained there for three days until the pursuers returned. Now the pursuers had sought them all along the road, but had not found them.

23 Then the two men returned and came down from the hill country and crossed over and came to Joshua the son of Nun, and they related to him all that had happened

Joshua
Chapter 2

to them.

24 They said to Joshua, "Surely the LORD has given all the land into our hands; moreover, all the inhabitants of the land have melted away before us."

Joshua
Chapter 2

Joshua
Chapter 3

JOSHUA 3
OBSERVATION WORKSHEET

Chapter Theme _____

THEN Joshua rose early in the morning; and he and all the sons of Israel set out from Shittim and came to the Jordan, and they lodged there before they crossed.

2 At the end of three days the officers went through the midst of the camp;

3 and they commanded the people, saying, "When you see the ark of the covenant of the LORD your God with the Levitical priests carrying it, then you shall set out from your place and go after it.

4 "However, there shall be between you and it a distance of about 2,000 cubits by measure. Do not come near it, that you may know the way by which you shall go, for you have not passed this way before."

5 Then Joshua said to the people, "Consecrate yourselves, for tomorrow the LORD will do wonders among you."

6 And Joshua spoke to the priests, saying, "Take up the ark of the covenant and cross over ahead of the people." So they took up the ark of the covenant and went ahead of the people.

7 Now the LORD said to Joshua, "This day I will begin to exalt you in the sight of all Israel, that they may know that just as I have been with Moses, I will be with you.

8 "You shall, moreover, command the priests who are carrying the ark of the covenant, saying, 'When you come to the edge of the waters of the Jordan, you shall stand still in the Jordan.'"

9 Then Joshua said to the sons of Israel, "Come here, and hear the words of the LORD your God."

10 Joshua said, "By this you shall know that the living God is among you, and that He will assuredly dispossess from before you the Canaanite, the Hittite, the Hivite, the Perizzite, the Girgashite, the Amorite, and the Jebusite.

11 "Behold, the ark of the covenant of the LORD of all the earth is crossing over ahead of you into the Jordan.

© 2008 Precept Ministries International

Joshua
Chapter 3

12 "Now then, take for yourselves twelve men from the tribes of Israel, one man for each tribe.

13 "It shall come about when the soles of the feet of the priests who carry the ark of the LORD, the LORD of all the earth, rest in the waters of the Jordan, the waters of the Jordan will be cut off, and the waters which are flowing down from above will stand in one heap."

14 So when the people set out from their tents to cross the Jordan with the priests carrying the ark of the covenant before the people,

15 and when those who carried the ark came into the Jordan, and the feet of the priests carrying the ark were dipped in the edge of the water (for the Jordan overflows all its banks all the days of harvest),

16 the waters which were flowing down from above stood and rose up in one heap, a great distance away at Adam, the city that is beside Zarethan; and those which were flowing down toward the sea of the Arabah, the Salt Sea, were completely cut off. So the people crossed opposite Jericho.

17 And the priests who carried the ark of the covenant of the LORD stood firm on dry ground in the middle of the Jordan while all Israel crossed on dry ground, until all the nation had finished crossing the Jordan.

Joshua
Chapter 4

JOSHUA 4
OBSERVATION WORKSHEET

Chapter Theme _____

NOW when all the nation had finished crossing the Jordan, the LORD spoke to Joshua, saying,

2 "Take for yourselves twelve men from the people, one man from each tribe,

3 and command them, saying, 'Take up for yourselves twelve stones from here out of the middle of the Jordan, from the place where the priests' feet are standing firm, and carry them over with you and lay them down in the lodging place where you will lodge tonight.'"

4 So Joshua called the twelve men whom he had appointed from the sons of Israel, one man from each tribe;

5 and Joshua said to them, "Cross again to the ark of the LORD your God into the middle of the Jordan, and each of you take up a stone on his shoulder, according to the number of the tribes of the sons of Israel.

6 "Let this be a sign among you, so that when your children ask later, saying, 'What do these stones mean to you?'

7 then you shall say to them, 'Because the waters of the Jordan were cut off before the ark of the covenant of the LORD; when it crossed the Jordan, the waters of the Jordan were cut off.' So these stones shall become a memorial to the sons of Israel forever."

8 Thus the sons of Israel did as Joshua commanded, and took up twelve stones from the middle of the Jordan, just as the LORD spoke to Joshua, according to the number of the tribes of the sons of Israel; and they carried them over with them to the lodging place and put them down there.

9 Then Joshua set up twelve stones in the middle of the Jordan at the place where the feet of the priests who carried the ark of the covenant were standing, and they are there to this day.

10 For the priests who carried the ark were standing in the middle of the Jordan until everything was completed that the LORD had commanded Joshua to speak to the

© 2008 Precept Ministries International

Joshua
Chapter 4

people, according to all that Moses had commanded Joshua. And the people hurried and crossed;

11 and when all the people had finished crossing, the ark of the LORD and the priests crossed before the people.

12 The sons of Reuben and the sons of Gad and the half-tribe of Manasseh crossed over in battle array before the sons of Israel, just as Moses had spoken to them;

13 about 40,000 equipped for war, crossed for battle before the LORD to the desert plains of Jericho.

14 On that day the LORD exalted Joshua in the sight of all Israel; so that they revered him, just as they had revered Moses all the days of his life.

15 Now the LORD said to Joshua,

16 "Command the priests who carry the ark of the testimony that they come up from the Jordan."

17 So Joshua commanded the priests, saying, "Come up from the Jordan."

18 It came about when the priests who carried the ark of the covenant of the LORD had come up from the middle of the Jordan, and the soles of the priests' feet were lifted up to the dry ground, that the waters of the Jordan returned to their place, and went over all its banks as before.

19 Now the people came up from the Jordan on the tenth of the first month and camped at Gilgal on the eastern edge of Jericho.

20 Those twelve stones which they had taken from the Jordan, Joshua set up at Gilgal.

21 He said to the sons of Israel, "When your children ask their fathers in time to come, saying, 'What are these stones?'

22 then you shall inform your children, saying, 'Israel crossed this Jordan on dry ground.'

23 "For the LORD your God dried up the waters of the Jordan before you until you had crossed, just as the LORD your God had done to the Red Sea, which He dried up before us until we had crossed;

24 that all the peoples of the earth may know that the hand of the LORD is mighty, so that you may fear the LORD your God forever.

Joshua
Chapter 5

JOSHUA 5
OBSERVATION WORKSHEET

Chapter Theme _____

NOW it came about when all the kings of the Amorites who were beyond the Jordan to the west, and all the kings of the Canaanites who were by the sea, heard how the LORD had dried up the waters of the Jordan before the sons of Israel until they had crossed, that their hearts melted, and there was no spirit in them any longer because of the sons of Israel.

2   At that time the LORD said to Joshua, "Make for yourself flint knives and circumcise again the sons of Israel the second time."

3   So Joshua made himself flint knives and circumcised the sons of Israel at Gibeath-haaraloth.

4   This is the reason why Joshua circumcised them: all the people who came out of Egypt who were males, all the men of war, died in the wilderness along the way after they came out of Egypt.

5   For all the people who came out were circumcised, but all the people who were born in the wilderness along the way as they came out of Egypt had not been circumcised.

6   For the sons of Israel walked forty years in the wilderness, until all the nation, that is, the men of war who came out of Egypt, perished because they did not listen to the voice of the LORD, to whom the LORD had sworn that He would not let them see the land which the LORD had sworn to their fathers to give us, a land flowing with milk and honey.

7   Their children whom He raised up in their place, Joshua circumcised; for they were uncircumcised, because they had not circumcised them along the way.

8   Now when they had finished circumcising all the nation, they remained in their places in the camp until they were healed.

9   Then the LORD said to Joshua, "Today I have rolled away the reproach of Egypt from you." So the name of that place is called Gilgal to this day.

10 While the sons of Israel camped at Gilgal they observed the Passover on the eve-

Joshua
Chapter 5

ning of the fourteenth day of the month on the desert plains of Jericho.

11 On the day after the Passover, on that very day, they ate some of the produce of the land, unleavened cakes and parched grain.

12 The manna ceased on the day after they had eaten some of the produce of the land, so that the sons of Israel no longer had manna, but they ate some of the yield of the land of Canaan during that year.

13 Now it came about when Joshua was by Jericho, that he lifted up his eyes and looked, and behold, a man was standing opposite him with his sword drawn in his hand, and Joshua went to him and said to him, "Are you for us or for our adversaries?"

14 He said, "No; rather I indeed come now as captain of the host of the LORD." And Joshua fell on his face to the earth, and bowed down, and said to him, "What has my LORD to say to his servant?"

15 The captain of the LORD's host said to Joshua, "Remove your sandals from your feet, for the place where you are standing is holy." And Joshua did so.

Joshua
Chapter 6

JOSHUA 6
OBSERVATION WORKSHEET

Chapter Theme ───────────────────────────────────────

NOW Jericho was tightly shut because of the sons of Israel; no one went out and no one came in.

2 The LORD said to Joshua, "See, I have given Jericho into your hand, with its king and the valiant warriors.

3 "You shall march around the city, all the men of war circling the city once. You shall do so for six days.

4 "Also seven priests shall carry seven trumpets of rams' horns before the ark; then on the seventh day you shall march around the city seven times, and the priests shall blow the trumpets.

5 "It shall be that when they make a long blast with the ram's horn, and when you hear the sound of the trumpet, all the people shall shout with a great shout; and the wall of the city will fall down flat, and the people will go up every man straight ahead."

6 So Joshua the son of Nun called the priests and said to them, "Take up the ark of the covenant, and let seven priests carry seven trumpets of rams' horns before the ark of the LORD."

7 Then he said to the people, "Go forward, and march around the city, and let the armed men go on before the ark of the LORD."

8 And it was so, that when Joshua had spoken to the people, the seven priests carrying the seven trumpets of rams' horns before the LORD went forward and blew the trumpets; and the ark of the covenant of the LORD followed them.

9 The armed men went before the priests who blew the trumpets, and the rear guard came after the ark, while they continued to blow the trumpets.

10 But Joshua commanded the people, saying, "You shall not shout nor let your voice be heard nor let a word proceed out of your mouth, until the day I tell you, 'Shout!' Then you shall shout!"

11 So he had the ark of the LORD taken around the city, circling it once; then they

Joshua
Chapter 6

came into the camp and spent the night in the camp.

12 Now Joshua rose early in the morning, and the priests took up the ark of the LORD.

13 The seven priests carrying the seven trumpets of rams' horns before the ark of the LORD went on continually, and blew the trumpets; and the armed men went before them and the rear guard came after the ark of the LORD, while they continued to blow the trumpets.

14 Thus the second day they marched around the city once and returned to the camp; they did so for six days.

15 Then on the seventh day they rose early at the dawning of the day and marched around the city in the same manner seven times; only on that day they marched around the city seven times.

16 At the seventh time, when the priests blew the trumpets, Joshua said to the people, "Shout! For the LORD has given you the city.

17 "The city shall be under the ban, it and all that is in it belongs to the LORD; only Rahab the harlot and all who are with her in the house shall live, because she hid the messengers whom we sent.

18 "But as for you, only keep yourselves from the things under the ban, so that you do not covet them and take some of the things under the ban, and make the camp of Israel accursed and bring trouble on it.

19 "But all the silver and gold and articles of bronze and iron are holy to the LORD; they shall go into the treasury of the LORD."

20 So the people shouted, and priests blew the trumpets; and when the people heard the sound of the trumpet, the people shouted with a great shout and the wall fell down flat, so that the people went up into the city, every man straight ahead, and they took the city.

21 They utterly destroyed everything in the city, both man and woman, young and old, and ox and sheep and donkey, with the edge of the sword.

22 Joshua said to the two men who had spied out the land, "Go into the harlot's house and bring the woman and all she has out of there, as you have sworn to her."

23 So the young men who were spies went in and brought out Rahab and her father and her mother and her brothers and all she had; they also brought out all her relatives

Joshua
Chapter 6

and placed them outside the camp of Israel.

24 They burned the city with fire, and all that was in it. Only the silver and gold, and articles of bronze and iron, they put into the treasury of the house of the LORD.

25 However, Rahab the harlot and her father's household and all she had, Joshua spared; and she has lived in the midst of Israel to this day, for she hid the messengers whom Joshua sent to spy out Jericho.

26 Then Joshua made them take an oath at that time, saying, "Cursed before the LORD is the man who rises up and builds this city Jericho; with the loss of his firstborn he shall lay its foundation, and with the loss of his youngest son he shall set up its gates."

27 So the LORD was with Joshua, and his fame was in all the land.

Joshua
Chapter 6

Joshua
Chapter 7

JOSHUA 7
OBSERVATION WORKSHEET

Chapter Theme _____

BUT the sons of Israel acted unfaithfully in regard to the things under the ban, for Achan, the son of Carmi, the son of Zabdi, the son of Zerah, from the tribe of Judah, took some of the things under the ban, therefore the anger of the LORD burned against the sons of Israel.

2 Now Joshua sent men from Jericho to Ai, which is near Beth-aven, east of Bethel, and said to them, "Go up and spy out the land." So the men went up and spied out Ai.

3 They returned to Joshua and said to him, "Do not let all the people go up; only about two or three thousand men need go up to Ai; do not make all the people toil up there, for they are few."

4 So about three thousand men from the people went up there, but they fled from the men of Ai.

5 The men of Ai struck down about thirty-six of their men, and pursued them from the gate as far as Shebarim and struck them down on the descent, so the hearts of the people melted and became as water.

6 Then Joshua tore his clothes and fell to the earth on his face before the ark of the LORD until the evening, both he and the elders of Israel; and they put dust on their heads.

7 Joshua said, "Alas, O LORD GOD, why did You ever bring this people over the Jordan, only to deliver us into the hand of the Amorites, to destroy us? If only we had been willing to dwell beyond the Jordan!

8 "O LORD, what can I say since Israel has turned their back before their enemies?

9 "For the Canaanites and all the inhabitants of the land will hear of it, and they will surround us and cut off our name from the earth. And what will You do for Your great name?"

10 So the LORD said to Joshua, "Rise up! Why is it that you have fallen on your

Joshua
Chapter 7

face?

11 "Israel has sinned, and they have also transgressed My covenant which I commanded them. And they have even taken some of the things under the ban and have both stolen and deceived. Moreover, they have also put them among their own things.

12 "Therefore the sons of Israel cannot stand before their enemies; they turn their backs before their enemies, for they have become accursed. I will not be with you anymore unless you destroy the things under the ban from your midst.

13 "Rise up! Consecrate the people and say, 'Consecrate yourselves for tomorrow, for thus the LORD, the God of Israel, has said, "There are things under the ban in your midst, O Israel. You cannot stand before your enemies until you have removed the things under the ban from your midst."

14 'In the morning then you shall come near by your tribes. And it shall be that the tribe which the LORD takes by lot shall come near by families, and the family which the LORD takes shall come near by households, and the household which the LORD takes shall come near man by man.

15 'It shall be that the one who is taken with the things under the ban shall be burned with fire, he and all that belongs to him, because he has transgressed the covenant of the LORD, and because he has committed a disgraceful thing in Israel.'"

16 So Joshua arose early in the morning and brought Israel near by tribes, and the tribe of Judah was taken.

17 He brought the family of Judah near, and he took the family of the Zerahites; and he brought the family of the Zerahites near man by man, and Zabdi was taken.

18 He brought his household near man by man; and Achan, son of Carmi, son of Zabdi, son of Zerah, from the tribe of Judah, was taken.

19 Then Joshua said to Achan, "My son, I implore you, give glory to the LORD, the God of Israel, and give praise to Him; and tell me now what you have done. Do not hide it from me."

20 So Achan answered Joshua and said, "Truly, I have sinned against the LORD, the God of Israel, and this is what I did:

21 when I saw among the spoil a beautiful mantle from Shinar and two hundred shekels of silver and a bar of gold fifty shekels in weight, then I coveted them and took

Joshua
Chapter 7

them; and behold, they are concealed in the earth inside my tent with the silver underneath it."

22 So Joshua sent messengers, and they ran to the tent; and behold, it was concealed in his tent with the silver underneath it.

23 They took them from inside the tent and brought them to Joshua and to all the sons of Israel, and they poured them out before the LORD.

24 Then Joshua and all Israel with him, took Achan the son of Zerah, the silver, the mantle, the bar of gold, his sons, his daughters, his oxen, his donkeys, his sheep, his tent and all that belonged to him; and they brought them up to the valley of Achor.

25 Joshua said, "Why have you troubled us? The LORD will trouble you this day." And all Israel stoned them with stones; and they burned them with fire after they had stoned them with stones.

26 They raised over him a great heap of stones that stands to this day, and the LORD turned from the fierceness of His anger. Therefore the name of that place has been called the valley of Achor to this day.

Joshua
Chapter 7

Joshua
Chapter 8

JOSHUA 8
OBSERVATION WORKSHEET

Chapter Theme _____

NOW the LORD said to Joshua, "Do not fear or be dismayed. Take all the people of war with you and arise, go up to Ai; see, I have given into your hand the king of Ai, his people, his city, and his land.

2 "You shall do to Ai and its king just as you did to Jericho and its king; you shall take only its spoil and its cattle as plunder for yourselves. Set an ambush for the city behind it."

3 So Joshua rose with all the people of war to go up to Ai; and Joshua chose 30,000 men, valiant warriors, and sent them out at night.

4 He commanded them, saying, "See, you are going to ambush the city from behind it. Do not go very far from the city, but all of you be ready.

5 "Then I and all the people who are with me will approach the city. And when they come out to meet us as at the first, we will flee before them.

6 "They will come out after us until we have drawn them away from the city, for they will say, 'They are fleeing before us as at the first.' So we will flee before them.

7 "And you shall rise from your ambush and take possession of the city, for the LORD your God will deliver it into your hand.

8 "Then it will be when you have seized the city, that you shall set the city on fire. You shall do it according to the word of the LORD. See, I have commanded you."

9 So Joshua sent them away, and they went to the place of ambush and remained between Bethel and Ai, on the west side of Ai; but Joshua spent that night among the people.

10 Now Joshua rose early in the morning and mustered the people, and he went up with the elders of Israel before the people to Ai.

11 Then all the people of war who were with him went up and drew near and arrived in front of the city, and camped on the north side of Ai. Now there was a valley between him and Ai.

Joshua
Chapter 8

12 And he took about 5,000 men and set them in ambush between Bethel and Ai, on the west side of the city.

13 So they stationed the people, all the army that was on the north side of the city, and its rear guard on the west side of the city, and Joshua spent that night in the midst of the valley.

14 It came about when the king of Ai saw it, that the men of the city hurried and rose up early and went out to meet Israel in battle, he and all his people at the appointed place before the desert plain. But he did not know that there was an ambush against him behind the city.

15 Joshua and all Israel pretended to be beaten before them, and fled by the way of the wilderness.

16 And all the people who were in the city were called together to pursue them, and they pursued Joshua and were drawn away from the city.

17 So not a man was left in Ai or Bethel who had not gone out after Israel, and they left the city unguarded and pursued Israel.

18 Then the LORD said to Joshua, "Stretch out the javelin that is in your hand toward Ai, for I will give it into your hand." So Joshua stretched out the javelin that was in his hand toward the city.

19 The men in ambush rose quickly from their place, and when he had stretched out his hand, they ran and entered the city and captured it, and they quickly set the city on fire.

20 When the men of Ai turned back and looked, behold, the smoke of the city ascended to the sky, and they had no place to flee this way or that, for the people who had been fleeing to the wilderness turned against the pursuers.

21 When Joshua and all Israel saw that the men in ambush had captured the city and that the smoke of the city ascended, they turned back and slew the men of Ai.

22 The others came out from the city to encounter them, so that they were trapped in the midst of Israel, some on this side and some on that side; and they slew them until no one was left of those who survived or escaped.

23 But they took alive the king of Ai and brought him to Joshua.

24 Now when Israel had finished killing all the inhabitants of Ai in the field in the wil-

Joshua
Chapter 8

derness where they pursued them, and all of them were fallen by the edge of the sword until they were destroyed, then all Israel returned to Ai and struck it with the edge of the sword.

25 All who fell that day, both men and women, were 12,000—all the people of Ai.

26 For Joshua did not withdraw his hand with which he stretched out the javelin until he had utterly destroyed all the inhabitants of Ai.

27 Israel took only the cattle and the spoil of that city as plunder for themselves, according to the word of the LORD which He had commanded Joshua.

28 So Joshua burned Ai and made it a heap forever, a desolation until this day.

29 He hanged the king of Ai on a tree until evening; and at sunset Joshua gave command and they took his body down from the tree and threw it at the entrance of the city gate, and raised over it a great heap of stones that stands to this day.

30 Then Joshua built an altar to the LORD, the God of Israel, in Mount Ebal,

31 just as Moses the servant of the LORD had commanded the sons of Israel, as it is written in the book of the law of Moses, an altar of uncut stones on which no man had wielded an iron tool; and they offered burnt offerings on it to the LORD, and sacrificed peace offerings.

32 He wrote there on the stones a copy of the law of Moses, which he had written, in the presence of the sons of Israel.

33 All Israel with their elders and officers and their judges were standing on both sides of the ark before the Levitical priests who carried the ark of the covenant of the LORD, the stranger as well as the native. Half of them stood in front of Mount Gerizim and half of them in front of Mount Ebal, just as Moses the servant of the LORD had given command at first to bless the people of Israel.

34 Then afterward he read all the words of the law, the blessing and the curse, according to all that is written in the book of the law.

35 There was not a word of all that Moses had commanded which Joshua did not read before all the assembly of Israel with the women and the little ones and the strangers who were living among them.

Joshua
Chapter 8

Joshua
Chapter 9

JOSHUA 9
OBSERVATION WORKSHEET

Chapter Theme _____

NOW it came about when all the kings who were beyond the Jordan, in the hill country and in the lowland and on all the coast of the Great Sea toward Lebanon, the Hittite and the Amorite, the Canaanite, the Perizzite, the Hivite and the Jebusite, heard of it,

2   that they gathered themselves together with one accord to fight with Joshua and with Israel.

3   When the inhabitants of Gibeon heard what Joshua had done to Jericho and to Ai,

4   they also acted craftily and set out as envoys, and took worn-out sacks on their donkeys, and wineskins worn-out and torn and mended,

5   and worn-out and patched sandals on their feet, and worn-out clothes on themselves; and all the bread of their provision was dry and had become crumbled.

6   They went to Joshua to the camp at Gilgal and said to him and to the men of Israel, "We have come from a far country; now therefore, make a covenant with us."

7   The men of Israel said to the Hivites, "Perhaps you are living within our land; how then shall we make a covenant with you?"

8   But they said to Joshua, "We are your servants." Then Joshua said to them, "Who are you and where do you come from?"

9   They said to him, "Your servants have come from a very far country because of the fame of the LORD your God; for we have heard the report of Him and all that He did in Egypt,

10 and all that He did to the two kings of the Amorites who were beyond the Jordan, to Sihon king of Heshbon and to Og king of Bashan who was at Ashtaroth.

11 "So our elders and all the inhabitants of our country spoke to us, saying, 'Take provisions in your hand for the journey, and go to meet them and say to them, "We are your servants; now then, make a covenant with us."'

12 This our bread was warm when we took it for our provisions out of our houses

© 2008 Precept Ministries International

Joshua
Chapter 9

on the day that we left to come to you; but now behold, it is dry and has become crumbled.

13 "These wineskins which we filled were new, and behold, they are torn; and these our clothes and our sandals are worn out because of the very long journey."

14 So the men of Israel took some of their provisions, and did not ask for the counsel of the LORD.

15 Joshua made peace with them and made a covenant with them, to let them live; and the leaders of the congregation swore an oath to them.

16 It came about at the end of three days after they had made a covenant with them, that they heard that they were neighbors and that they were living within their land.

17 Then the sons of Israel set out and came to their cities on the third day. Now their cities were Gibeon and Chephirah and Beeroth and Kiriath-jearim.

18 The sons of Israel did not strike them because the leaders of the congregation had sworn to them by the LORD the God of Israel. And the whole congregation grumbled against the leaders.

19 But all the leaders said to the whole congregation, "We have sworn to them by the LORD, the God of Israel, and now we cannot touch them.

20 "This we will do to them, even let them live, so that wrath will not be upon us for the oath which we swore to them."

21 The leaders said to them, "Let them live." So they became hewers of wood and drawers of water for the whole congregation, just as the leaders had spoken to them.

22 Then Joshua called for them and spoke to them, saying, "Why have you deceived us, saying, 'We are very far from you,' when you are living within our land?

23 "Now therefore, you are cursed, and you shall never cease being slaves, both hewers of wood and drawers of water for the house of my God."

24 So they answered Joshua and said, "Because it was certainly told your servants that the LORD your God had commanded His servant Moses to give you all the land, and to destroy all the inhabitants of the land before you; therefore we feared greatly for our lives because of you, and have done this thing.

25 "Now behold, we are in your hands; do as it seems good and right in your sight to

Joshua
Chapter 9

do to us."

26 Thus he did to them, and delivered them from the hands of the sons of Israel, and they did not kill them.

27 But Joshua made them that day hewers of wood and drawers of water for the congregation and for the altar of the LORD, to this day, in the place which He would choose.

Joshua
Chapter 9

Joshua
Chapter 10

JOSHUA 10
OBSERVATION WORKSHEET

Chapter Theme _____

NOW it came about when Adoni-zedek king of Jerusalem heard that Joshua had captured Ai, and had utterly destroyed it (just as he had done to Jericho and its king, so he had done to Ai and its king), and that the inhabitants of Gibeon had made peace with Israel and were within their land,

2 that he feared greatly, because Gibeon was a great city, like one of the royal cities, and because it was greater than Ai, and all its men were mighty.

3 Therefore Adoni-zedek king of Jerusalem sent word to Hoham king of Hebron and to Piram king of Jarmuth and to Japhia king of Lachish and to Debir king of Eglon, saying,

4 "Come up to me and help me, and let us attack Gibeon, for it has made peace with Joshua and with the sons of Israel."

5 So the five kings of the Amorites, the king of Jerusalem, the king of Hebron, the king of Jarmuth, the king of Lachish, and the king of Eglon, gathered together and went up, they with all their armies, and camped by Gibeon and fought against it.

6 Then the men of Gibeon sent word to Joshua to the camp at Gilgal, saying, "Do not abandon your servants; come up to us quickly and save us and help us, for all the kings of the Amorites that live in the hill country have assembled against us."

7 So Joshua went up from Gilgal, he and all the people of war with him and all the valiant warriors.

8 The LORD said to Joshua, "Do not fear them, for I have given them into your hands; not one of them shall stand before you."

9 So Joshua came upon them suddenly by marching all night from Gilgal.

10 And the LORD confounded them before Israel, and He slew them with a great slaughter at Gibeon, and pursued them by the way of the ascent of Beth-horon and struck them as far as Azekah and Makkedah.

11 As they fled from before Israel, while they were at the descent of Beth-horon, the

Joshua
Chapter 10

LORD threw large stones from heaven on them as far as Azekah, and they died; there were more who died from the hailstones than those whom the sons of Israel killed with the sword.

12 Then Joshua spoke to the LORD in the day when the LORD delivered up the Amorites before the sons of Israel, and he said in the sight of Israel,

"O sun, stand still at Gibeon,

And O moon in the valley of Aijalon."

13 So the sun stood still, and the moon stopped,

Until the nation avenged themselves of their enemies.

Is it not written in the book of Jashar? And the sun stopped in the middle of the sky and did not hasten to go down for about a whole day.

14 There was no day like that before it or after it, when the LORD listened to the voice of a man; for the LORD fought for Israel.

15 Then Joshua and all Israel with him returned to the camp to Gilgal.

16 Now these five kings had fled and hidden themselves in the cave at Makkedah.

17 It was told Joshua, saying, "The five kings have been found hidden in the cave at Makkedah."

18 Joshua said, "Roll large stones against the mouth of the cave, and assign men by it to guard them,

19 but do not stay there yourselves; pursue your enemies and attack them in the rear. Do not allow them to enter their cities, for the LORD your God has delivered them into your hand."

20 It came about when Joshua and the sons of Israel had finished slaying them with a very great slaughter, until they were destroyed, and the survivors who remained of them had entered the fortified cities,

21 that all the people returned to the camp to Joshua at Makkedah in peace. No one uttered a word against any of the sons of Israel.

22 Then Joshua said, "Open the mouth of the cave and bring these five kings out to me from the cave."

23 They did so, and brought these five kings out to him from the cave: the king of Jerusalem, the king of Hebron, the king of Jarmuth, the king of Lachish, and the king of Eglon.

Joshua
Chapter 10

24 When they brought these kings out to Joshua, Joshua called for all the men of Israel, and said to the chiefs of the men of war who had gone with him, "Come near, put your feet on the necks of these kings." So they came near and put their feet on their necks.

25 Joshua then said to them, "Do not fear or be dismayed! Be strong and courageous, for thus the LORD will do to all your enemies with whom you fight."

26 So afterward Joshua struck them and put them to death, and he hanged them on five trees; and they hung on the trees until evening.

27 It came about at sunset that Joshua gave a command, and they took them down from the trees and threw them into the cave where they had hidden themselves, and put large stones over the mouth of the cave, to this very day.

28 Now Joshua captured Makkedah on that day, and struck it and its king with the edge of the sword; he utterly destroyed it and every person who was in it. He left no survivor. Thus he did to the king of Makkedah just as he had done to the king of Jericho.

29 Then Joshua and all Israel with him passed on from Makkedah to Libnah, and fought against Libnah.

30 The LORD gave it also with its king into the hands of Israel, and he struck it and every person who was in it with the edge of the sword. He left no survivor in it. Thus he did to its king just as he had done to the king of Jericho.

31 And Joshua and all Israel with him passed on from Libnah to Lachish, and they camped by it and fought against it.

32 The LORD gave Lachish into the hands of Israel; and he captured it on the second day, and struck it and every person who was in it with the edge of the sword, according to all that he had done to Libnah.

33 Then Horam king of Gezer came up to help Lachish, and Joshua defeated him and his people until he had left him no survivor.

34 And Joshua and all Israel with him passed on from Lachish to Eglon, and they camped by it and fought against it.

35 They captured it on that day and struck it with the edge of the sword; and he utterly destroyed that day every person who was in it, according to all that he had done to

Joshua
Chapter 10

Lachish.

36 Then Joshua and all Israel with him went up from Eglon to Hebron, and they fought against it.

37 They captured it and struck it and its king and all its cities and all the persons who were in it with the edge of the sword. He left no survivor, according to all that he had done to Eglon. And he utterly destroyed it and every person who was in it.

38 Then Joshua and all Israel with him returned to Debir, and they fought against it.

39 He captured it and its king and all its cities, and they struck them with the edge of the sword, and utterly destroyed every person who was in it. He left no survivor. Just as he had done to Hebron, so he did to Debir and its king, as he had also done to Libnah and its king.

40 Thus Joshua struck all the land, the hill country and the Negev and the lowland and the slopes and all their kings. He left no survivor, but he utterly destroyed all who breathed, just as the LORD, the God of Israel, had commanded.

41 Joshua struck them from Kadesh-barnea even as far as Gaza, and all the country of Goshen even as far as Gibeon.

42 Joshua captured all these kings and their lands at one time, because the LORD, the God of Israel, fought for Israel.

43 So Joshua and all Israel with him returned to the camp at Gilgal.

Joshua
Chapter 11

JOSHUA 11
OBSERVATION WORKSHEET

Chapter Theme _____

THEN it came about, when Jabin king of Hazor heard of it, that he sent to Jobab king of Madon and to the king of Shimron and to the king of Achshaph,

2   and to the kings who were of the north in the hill country, and in the Arabah—south of Chinneroth and in the lowland and on the heights of Dor on the west—

3   to the Canaanite on the east and on the west, and the Amorite and the Hittite and the Perizzite and the Jebusite in the hill country, and the Hivite at the foot of Hermon in the land of Mizpeh.

4   They came out, they and all their armies with them, as many people as the sand that is on the seashore, with very many horses and chariots.

5   So all of these kings having agreed to meet, came and encamped together at the waters of Merom, to fight against Israel.

6   Then the LORD said to Joshua, "Do not be afraid because of them, for tomorrow at this time I will deliver all of them slain before Israel; you shall hamstring their horses and burn their chariots with fire."

7   So Joshua and all the people of war with him came upon them suddenly by the waters of Merom, and attacked them.

8   The LORD delivered them into the hand of Israel, so that they defeated them, and pursued them as far as Great Sidon and Misrephoth-maim and the valley of Mizpeh to the east; and they struck them until no survivor was left to them.

9   Joshua did to them as the LORD had told him; he hamstrung their horses and burned their chariots with fire.

10 Then Joshua turned back at that time, and captured Hazor and struck its king with the sword; for Hazor formerly was the head of all these kingdoms.

11 They struck every person who was in it with the edge of the sword, utterly destroying them; there was no one left who breathed. And he burned Hazor with fire.

12 Joshua captured all the cities of these kings, and all their kings, and he struck them with the edge of the sword, and utterly destroyed them; just as Moses the servant

Joshua
Chapter 11

of the LORD had commanded.

13 However, Israel did not burn any cities that stood on their mounds, except Hazor alone, which Joshua burned.

14 All the spoil of these cities and the cattle, the sons of Israel took as their plunder; but they struck every man with the edge of the sword, until they had destroyed them. They left no one who breathed.

15 Just as the LORD had commanded Moses his servant, so Moses commanded Joshua, and so Joshua did; he left nothing undone of all that the LORD had commanded Moses.

16 Thus Joshua took all that land: the hill country and all the Negev, all that land of Goshen, the lowland, the Arabah, the hill country of Israel and its lowland

17 from Mount Halak, that rises toward Seir, even as far as Baal-gad in the valley of Lebanon at the foot of Mount Hermon. And he captured all their kings and struck them down and put them to death.

18 Joshua waged war a long time with all these kings.

19 There was not a city which made peace with the sons of Israel except the Hivites living in Gibeon; they took them all in battle.

20 For it was of the LORD to harden their hearts, to meet Israel in battle in order that he might utterly destroy them, that they might receive no mercy, but that he might destroy them, just as the LORD had commanded Moses.

21 Then Joshua came at that time and cut off the Anakim from the hill country, from Hebron, from Debir, from Anab and from all the hill country of Judah and from all the hill country of Israel. Joshua utterly destroyed them with their cities.

22 There were no Anakim left in the land of the sons of Israel; only in Gaza, in Gath, and in Ashdod some remained.

23 So Joshua took the whole land, according to all that the LORD had spoken to Moses, and Joshua gave it for an inheritance to Israel according to their divisions by their tribes. Thus the land had rest from war.

© 2008 Precept Ministries International

Joshua
Chapter 12

JOSHUA 12
OBSERVATION WORKSHEET

Chapter Theme _____

NOW these are the kings of the land whom the sons of Israel defeated, and whose land they possessed beyond the Jordan toward the sunrise, from the valley of the Arnon as far as Mount Hermon, and all the Arabah to the east:

2 Sihon king of the Amorites, who lived in Heshbon, and ruled from Aroer, which is on the edge of the valley of the Arnon, both the middle of the valley and half of Gilead, even as far as the brook Jabbok, the border of the sons of Ammon;

3 and the Arabah as far as the Sea of Chinneroth toward the east, and as far as the sea of the Arabah, even the Salt Sea, eastward toward Beth-jeshimoth, and on the south, at the foot of the slopes of Pisgah;

4 and the territory of Og king of Bashan, one of the remnant of Rephaim, who lived at Ashtaroth and at Edrei,

5 and ruled over Mount Hermon and Salecah and all Bashan, as far as the border of the Geshurites and the Maacathites, and half of Gilead, as far as the border of Sihon king of Heshbon.

6 Moses the servant of the LORD and the sons of Israel defeated them; and Moses the servant of the LORD gave it to the Reubenites and the Gadites and the half-tribe of Manasseh as a possession.

7 Now these are the kings of the land whom Joshua and the sons of Israel defeated beyond the Jordan toward the west, from Baal-gad in the valley of Lebanon even as far as Mount Halak, which rises toward Seir; and Joshua gave it to the tribes of Israel as a possession according to their divisions,

8 in the hill country, in the lowland, in the Arabah, on the slopes, and in the wilderness, and in the Negev; the Hittite, the Amorite and the Canaanite, the Perizzite, the Hivite and the Jebusite:

9 the king of Jericho, one; the king of Ai, which is beside Bethel, one;

10 the king of Jerusalem, one; the king of Hebron, one;

11 the king of Jarmuth, one; the king of Lachish, one;

© 2008 Precept Ministries International

Joshua
Chapter 12

12 the king of Eglon, one; the king of Gezer, one;

13 the king of Debir, one; the king of Geder, one;

14 the king of Hormah, one; the king of Arad, one;

15 the king of Libnah, one; the king of Adullam, one;

16 the king of Makkedah, one; the king of Bethel, one;

17 the king of Tappuah, one; the king of Hepher, one;

18 the king of Aphek, one; the king of Lasharon, one;

19 the king of Madon, one; the king of Hazor, one;

20 the king of Shimron-meron, one; the king of Achshaph, one;

21 the king of Taanach, one; the king of Megiddo, one;

22 the king of Kedesh, one; the king of Jokneam in Carmel, one;

23 the king of Dor in the heights of Dor, one; the king of Goiim in Gilgal, one;

24 the king of Tirzah, one: in all, thirty-one kings.

Joshua
Chapter 13

JOSHUA 13
OBSERVATION WORKSHEET

Chapter Theme _____

NOW Joshua was old and advanced in years when the LORD said to him, "You are old and advanced in years, and very much of the land remains to be possessed.

2 "This is the land that remains: all the regions of the Philistines and all those of the Geshurites;

3 from the Shihor which is east of Egypt, even as far as the border of Ekron to the north (it is counted as Canaanite); the five LORDs of the Philistines: the Gazite, the Ashdodite, the Ashkelonite, the Gittite, the Ekronite; and the Avvite

4 to the south, all the land of the Canaanite, and Mearah that belongs to the Sidonians, as far as Aphek, to the border of the Amorite;

5 and the land of the Gebalite, and all of Lebanon, toward the east, from Baal-gad below Mount Hermon as far as Lebo-hamath.

6 "All the inhabitants of the hill country from Lebanon as far as Misrephoth-maim, all the Sidonians, I will drive them out from before the sons of Israel; only allot it to Israel for an inheritance as I have commanded you.

7 "Now therefore, apportion this land for an inheritance to the nine tribes and the half-tribe of Manasseh."

8 With the other half-tribe, the Reubenites and the Gadites received their inheritance which Moses gave them beyond the Jordan to the east, just as Moses the servant of the LORD gave to them;

9 from Aroer, which is on the edge of the valley of the Arnon, with the city which is in the middle of the valley, and all the plain of Medeba, as far as Dibon;

10 and all the cities of Sihon king of the Amorites, who reigned in Heshbon, as far as the border of the sons of Ammon;

11 and Gilead, and the territory of the Geshurites and Maacathites, and all Mount Hermon, and all Bashan as far as Salecah;

12 all the kingdom of Og in Bashan, who reigned in Ashtaroth and in Edrei (he alone

© 2008 Precept Ministries International

Joshua
Chapter 13

was left of the remnant of the Rephaim); for Moses struck them and dispossessed them.

13 But the sons of Israel did not dispossess the Geshurites or the Maacathites; for Geshur and Maacath live among Israel until this day.

14 Only to the tribe of Levi he did not give an inheritance; the offerings by fire to the LORD, the God of Israel, are their inheritance, as He spoke to him.

15 So Moses gave an inheritance to the tribe of the sons of Reuben according to their families.

16 Their territory was from Aroer, which is on the edge of the valley of the Arnon, with the city which is in the middle of the valley and all the plain by Medeba;

17 Heshbon, and all its cities which are on the plain: Dibon and Bamoth-baal and Beth-baal-meon,

18 and Jahaz and Kedemoth and Mephaath,

19 and Kiriathaim and Sibmah and Zereth-shahar on the hill of the valley,

20 and Beth-peor and the slopes of Pisgah and Beth-jeshimoth,

21 even all the cities of the plain and all the kingdom of Sihon king of the Amorites who reigned in Heshbon, whom Moses struck with the chiefs of Midian, Evi and Rekem and Zur and Hur and Reba, the princes of Sihon, who lived in the land.

22 The sons of Israel also killed Balaam the son of Beor, the diviner, with the sword among the rest of their slain.

23 The border of the sons of Reuben was the Jordan. This was the inheritance of the sons of Reuben according to their families, the cities and their villages.

24 Moses also gave an inheritance to the tribe of Gad, to the sons of Gad, according to their families.

25 Their territory was Jazer, and all the cities of Gilead, and half the land of the sons of Ammon, as far as Aroer which is before Rabbah;

26 and from Heshbon as far as Ramath-mizpeh and Betonim, and from Mahanaim as far as the border of Debir;

27 and in the valley, Beth-haram and Beth-nimrah and Succoth and Zaphon, the rest of the kingdom of Sihon king of Heshbon, with the Jordan as a border, as far as the lower end of the Sea of Chinnereth beyond the Jordan to the east.

Joshua
Chapter 13

28 This is the inheritance of the sons of Gad according to their families, the cities and their villages.

29 Moses also gave an inheritance to the half-tribe of Manasseh; and it was for the half-tribe of the sons of Manasseh according to their families.

30 Their territory was from Mahanaim, all Bashan, all the kingdom of Og king of Bashan, and all the towns of Jair, which are in Bashan, sixty cities;

31 also half of Gilead, with Ashtaroth and Edrei, the cities of the kingdom of Og in Bashan, were for the sons of Machir the son of Manasseh, for half of the sons of Machir according to their families.

32 These are the territories which Moses apportioned for an inheritance in the plains of Moab, beyond the Jordan at Jericho to the east.

33 But to the tribe of Levi, Moses did not give an inheritance; the LORD, the God of Israel, is their inheritance, as He had promised to them.

Joshua
Chapter 13

Joshua
Chapter 14

JOSHUA 14
OBSERVATION WORKSHEET

Chapter Theme _____

NOW these are the territories which the sons of Israel inherited in the land of Canaan, which Eleazar the priest, and Joshua the son of Nun, and the heads of the households of the tribes of the sons of Israel apportioned to them for an inheritance,

2 by the lot of their inheritance, as the LORD commanded through Moses, for the nine tribes and the half-tribe.

3 For Moses had given the inheritance of the two tribes and the half-tribe beyond the Jordan; but he did not give an inheritance to the Levites among them.

4 For the sons of Joseph were two tribes, Manasseh and Ephraim, and they did not give a portion to the Levites in the land, except cities to live in, with their pasture lands for their livestock and for their property.

5 Thus the sons of Israel did just as the LORD had commanded Moses, and they divided the land.

6 Then the sons of Judah drew near to Joshua in Gilgal, and Caleb the son of Jephunneh the Kenizzite said to him, "You know the word which the LORD spoke to Moses the man of God concerning you and me in Kadesh-barnea.

7 "I was forty years old when Moses the servant of the LORD sent me from Kadesh-barnea to spy out the land, and I brought word back to him as it was in my heart.

8 "Nevertheless my brethren who went up with me made the heart of the people melt with fear; but I followed the LORD my God fully.

9 "So Moses swore on that day, saying, 'Surely the land on which your foot has trodden will be an inheritance to you and to your children forever, because you have followed the LORD my God fully.'

10 "Now behold, the LORD has let me live, just as He spoke, these forty-five years, from the time that the LORD spoke this word to Moses, when Israel walked in the wilderness; and now behold, I am eighty-five years old today.

11 "I am still as strong today as I was in the day Moses sent me; as my strength was

Joshua
Chapter 14

then, so my strength is now, for war and for going out and coming in.

12 "Now then, give me this hill country about which the LORD spoke on that day, for you heard on that day that Anakim were there, with great fortified cities; perhaps the LORD will be with me, and I will drive them out as the LORD has spoken."

13 So Joshua blessed him and gave Hebron to Caleb the son of Jephunneh for an inheritance.

14 Therefore, Hebron became the inheritance of Caleb the son of Jephunneh the Kenizzite until this day, because he followed the LORD God of Israel fully.

15 Now the name of Hebron was formerly Kiriath-arba; for Arba was the greatest man among the Anakim. Then the land had rest from war.

Joshua
Chapter 15

JOSHUA 15
OBSERVATION WORKSHEET

Chapter Theme _____

NOW the lot for the tribe of the sons of Judah according to their families reached the border of Edom, southward to the wilderness of Zin at the extreme south.

2 Their south border was from the lower end of the Salt Sea, from the bay that turns to the south.

3 Then it proceeded southward to the ascent of Akrabbim and continued to Zin, then went up by the south of Kadesh-barnea and continued to Hezron, and went up to Addar and turned about to Karka.

4 It continued to Azmon and proceeded to the brook of Egypt, and the border ended at the sea. This shall be your south border.

5 The east border was the Salt Sea, as far as the mouth of the Jordan. And the border of the north side was from the bay of the sea at the mouth of the Jordan.

6 Then the border went up to Beth-hoglah, and continued on the north of Beth-arabah, and the border went up to the stone of Bohan the son of Reuben.

7 The border went up to Debir from the valley of Achor, and turned northward toward Gilgal which is opposite the ascent of Adummim, which is on the south of the valley; and the border continued to the waters of En-shemesh and it ended at En-rogel.

8 Then the border went up the valley of Ben-hinnom to the slope of the Jebusite on the south (that is, Jerusalem); and the border went up to the top of the mountain which is before the valley of Hinnom to the west, which is at the end of the valley of Rephaim toward the north.

9 From the top of the mountain the border curved to the spring of the waters of Nephtoah and proceeded to the cities of Mount Ephron, then the border curved to Baalah (that is, Kiriath-jearim).

10 The border turned about from Baalah westward to Mount Seir, and continued to the slope of Mount Jearim on the north (that is, Chesalon), and went down to Beth-

© 2008 Precept Ministries International

Joshua
Chapter 15

shemesh and continued through Timnah.

11 The border proceeded to the side of Ekron northward. Then the border curved to Shikkeron and continued to Mount Baalah and proceeded to Jabneel, and the border ended at the sea.

12 The west border was at the Great Sea, even its coastline. This is the border around the sons of Judah according to their families.

13 Now he gave to Caleb the son of Jephunneh a portion among the sons of Judah, according to the command of the LORD to Joshua, namely, Kiriath-arba, Arba being the father of Anak (that is, Hebron).

14 Caleb drove out from there the three sons of Anak: Sheshai and Ahiman and Talmai, the children of Anak.

15 Then he went up from there against the inhabitants of Debir; now the name of Debir formerly was Kiriath-sepher.

16 And Caleb said, "The one who attacks Kiriath-sepher and captures it, I will give him Achsah my daughter as a wife."

17 Othniel the son of Kenaz, the brother of Caleb, captured it; so he gave him Achsah his daughter as a wife.

18 It came about that when she came to him, she persuaded him to ask her father for a field. So she alighted from the donkey, and Caleb said to her, "What do you want?"

19 Then she said, "Give me a blessing; since you have given me the land of the Negev, give me also springs of water." So he gave her the upper springs and the lower springs.

20 This is the inheritance of the tribe of the sons of Judah according to their families.

21 Now the cities at the extremity of the tribe of the sons of Judah toward the border of Edom in the south were Kabzeel and Eder and Jagur,

22 and Kinah and Dimonah and Adadah,

23 and Kedesh and Hazor and Ithnan,

24 Ziph and Telem and Bealoth,

25 and Hazor-hadattah and Kerioth-hezron (that is, Hazor),

26 Amam and Shema and Moladah,

27 and Hazar-gaddah and Heshmon and Beth-pelet,

Joshua
Chapter 15

28 and Hazar-shual and Beersheba and Biziothiah,

29 Baalah and Iim and Ezem,

30 and Eltolad and Chesil and Hormah,

31 and Ziklag and Madmannah and Sansannah,

32 and Lebaoth and Shilhim and Ain and Rimmon; in all, twenty-nine cities with their villages.

33 In the lowland: Eshtaol and Zorah and Ashnah,

34 and Zanoah and En-gannim, Tappuah and Enam,

35 Jarmuth and Adullam, Socoh and Azekah,

36 and Shaaraim and Adithaim and Gederah and Gederothaim; fourteen cities with their villages.

37 Zenan and Hadashah and Migdal-gad,

38 and Dilean and Mizpeh and Joktheel,

39 Lachish and Bozkath and Eglon,

40 and Cabbon and Lahmas and Chitlish,

41 and Gederoth, Beth-dagon and Naamah and Makkedah; sixteen cities with their villages.

42 Libnah and Ether and Ashan,

43 and Iphtah and Ashnah and Nezib,

44 and Keilah and Achzib and Mareshah; nine cities with their villages.

45 Ekron, with its towns and its villages;

46 from Ekron even to the sea, all that were by the side of Ashdod, with their villages.

47 Ashdod, its towns and its villages; Gaza, its towns and its villages; as far as the brook of Egypt and the Great Sea, even its coastline.

48 In the hill country: Shamir and Jattir and Socoh,

49 and Dannah and Kiriath-sannah (that is, Debir),

50 and Anab and Eshtemoh and Anim,

51 and Goshen and Holon and Giloh; eleven cities with their villages.

52 Arab and Dumah and Eshan,

53 and Janum and Beth-tappuah and Aphekah,

54 and Humtah and Kiriath-arba (that is, Hebron), and Zior; nine cities with their vil-

Joshua
Chapter 15

lages.

55 Maon, Carmel and Ziph and Juttah,

56 and Jezreel and Jokdeam and Zanoah,

57 Kain, Gibeah and Timnah; ten cities with their villages.

58 Halhul, Beth-zur and Gedor,

59 and Maarath and Beth-anoth and Eltekon; six cities with their villages.

60 Kiriath-baal (that is, Kiriath-jearim), and Rabbah; two cities with their villages.

61 In the wilderness: Beth-arabah, Middin and Secacah,

62 and Nibshan and the City of Salt and Engedi; six cities with their villages.

63 Now as for the Jebusites, the inhabitants of Jerusalem, the sons of Judah could not drive them out; so the Jebusites live with the sons of Judah at Jerusalem until this day.

Joshua
Chapter 16

JOSHUA 16
OBSERVATION WORKSHEET

Chapter Theme ─────────────────────────

THEN the lot for the sons of Joseph went from the Jordan at Jericho to the waters of Jericho on the east into the wilderness, going up from Jericho through the hill country to Bethel.

2   It went from Bethel to Luz, and continued to the border of the Archites at Ataroth.

3   It went down westward to the territory of the Japhletites, as far as the territory of lower Beth-horon even to Gezer, and it ended at the sea.

4   The sons of Joseph, Manasseh and Ephraim, received their inheritance.

5   Now this was the territory of the sons of Ephraim according to their families: the border of their inheritance eastward was Ataroth-addar, as far as upper Beth-horon.

6   Then the border went westward at Michmethath on the north, and the border turned about eastward to Taanath-shiloh and continued beyond it to the east of Janoah.

7   It went down from Janoah to Ataroth and to Naarah, then reached Jericho and came out at the Jordan.

8   From Tappuah the border continued westward to the brook of Kanah, and it ended at the sea. This is the inheritance of the tribe of the sons of Ephraim according to their families,

9   together with the cities which were set apart for the sons of Ephraim in the midst of the inheritance of the sons of Manasseh, all the cities with their villages.

10 But they did not drive out the Canaanites who lived in Gezer, so the Canaanites live in the midst of Ephraim to this day, and they became forced laborers.

© 2008 Precept Ministries International

Joshua
Chapter 16

Joshua
Chapter 17

JOSHUA 17
OBSERVATION WORKSHEET

Chapter Theme _____

NOW this was the lot for the tribe of Manasseh, for he was the firstborn of Joseph. To Machir the firstborn of Manasseh, the father of Gilead, were allotted Gilead and Bashan, because he was a man of war.

2 So the lot was made for the rest of the sons of Manasseh according to their families: for the sons of Abiezer and for the sons of Helek and for the sons of Asriel and for the sons of Shechem and for the sons of Hepher and for the sons of Shemida; these were the male descendants of Manasseh the son of Joseph according to their families.

3 However, Zelophehad, the son of Hepher, the son of Gilead, the son of Machir, the son of Manasseh, had no sons, only daughters; and these are the names of his daughters: Mahlah and Noah, Hoglah, Milcah and Tirzah.

4 They came near before Eleazar the priest and before Joshua the son of Nun and before the leaders, saying, "The LORD commanded Moses to give us an inheritance among our brothers." So according to the command of the LORD he gave them an inheritance among their father's brothers.

5 Thus there fell ten portions to Manasseh, besides the land of Gilead and Bashan, which is beyond the Jordan,

6 because the daughters of Manasseh received an inheritance among his sons. And the land of Gilead belonged to the rest of the sons of Manasseh.

7 The border of Manasseh ran from Asher to Michmethath which was east of Shechem; then the border went southward to the inhabitants of En-tappuah.

8 The land of Tappuah belonged to Manasseh, but Tappuah on the border of Manasseh belonged to the sons of Ephraim.

9 The border went down to the brook of Kanah, southward of the brook (these cities belonged to Ephraim among the cities of Manasseh), and the border of Manasseh was on the north side of the brook and it ended at the sea.

10 The south side belonged to Ephraim and the north side to Manasseh, and the sea

© 2008 Precept Ministries International

Joshua
Chapter 17

was their border; and they reached to Asher on the north and to Issachar on the east.

11 In Issachar and in Asher, Manasseh had Beth-shean and its towns and Ibleam and its towns, and the inhabitants of Dor and its towns, and the inhabitants of En-dor and its towns, and the inhabitants of Taanach and its towns, and the inhabitants of Megiddo and its towns, the third is Napheth.

12 But the sons of Manasseh could not take possession of these cities, because the Canaanites persisted in living in that land.

13 It came about when the sons of Israel became strong, they put the Canaanites to forced labor, but they did not drive them out completely.

14 Then the sons of Joseph spoke to Joshua, saying, "Why have you given me only one lot and one portion for an inheritance, since I am a numerous people whom the LORD has thus far blessed?"

15 Joshua said to them, "If you are a numerous people, go up to the forest and clear a place for yourself there in the land of the Perizzites and of the Rephaim, since the hill country of Ephraim is too narrow for you."

16 The sons of Joseph said, "The hill country is not enough for us, and all the Canaanites who live in the valley land have chariots of iron, both those who are in Beth-shean and its towns and those who are in the valley of Jezreel."

17 Joshua spoke to the house of Joseph, to Ephraim and Manasseh, saying, "You are a numerous people and have great power; you shall not have one lot only,

18 but the hill country shall be yours. For though it is a forest, you shall clear it, and to its farthest borders it shall be yours; for you shall drive out the Canaanites, even though they have chariots of iron and though they are strong."

JOSHUA 18
OBSERVATION WORKSHEET

Chapter Theme _____

THEN the whole congregation of the sons of Israel assembled themselves at Shiloh, and set up the tent of meeting there; and the land was subdued before them.

2 There remained among the sons of Israel seven tribes who had not divided their inheritance.

3 So Joshua said to the sons of Israel, "How long will you put off entering to take possession of the land which the LORD, the God of your fathers, has given you?

4 "Provide for yourselves three men from each tribe that I may send them, and that they may arise and walk through the land and write a description of it according to their inheritance; then they shall return to me.

5 "They shall divide it into seven portions; Judah shall stay in its territory on the south, and the house of Joseph shall stay in their territory on the north.

6 "You shall describe the land in seven divisions, and bring the description here to me. I will cast lots for you here before the LORD our God.

7 "For the Levites have no portion among you, because the priesthood of the LORD is their inheritance. Gad and Reuben and the half-tribe of Manasseh also have received their inheritance eastward beyond the Jordan, which Moses the servant of the LORD gave them."

8 Then the men arose and went, and Joshua commanded those who went to describe the land, saying, "Go and walk through the land and describe it, and return to me; then I will cast lots for you here before the LORD in Shiloh."

9 So the men went and passed through the land, and described it by cities in seven divisions in a book; and they came to Joshua to the camp at Shiloh.

10 And Joshua cast lots for them in Shiloh before the LORD, and there Joshua divided the land to the sons of Israel according to their divisions.

11 Now the lot of the tribe of the sons of Benjamin came up according to their families, and the territory of their lot lay between the sons of Judah and the sons of Joseph.

Joshua
Chapter 18

12 Their border on the north side was from the Jordan, then the border went up to the side of Jericho on the north, and went up through the hill country westward, and it ended at the wilderness of Beth-aven.

13 From there the border continued to Luz, to the side of Luz (that is, Bethel) southward; and the border went down to Ataroth-addar, near the hill which lies on the south of lower Beth-horon.

14 The border extended from there and turned round on the west side southward, from the hill which lies before Beth-horon southward; and it ended at Kiriath-baal (that is, Kiriath-jearim), a city of the sons of Judah. This was the west side.

15 Then the south side was from the edge of Kiriath-jearim, and the border went westward and went to the fountain of the waters of Nephtoah.

16 The border went down to the edge of the hill which is in the valley of Ben-hinnom, which is in the valley of Rephaim northward; and it went down to the valley of Hinnom, to the slope of the Jebusite southward, and went down to En-rogel.

17 It extended northward and went to En-shemesh and went to Geliloth, which is opposite the ascent of Adummim, and it went down to the stone of Bohan the son of Reuben.

18 It continued to the side in front of the Arabah northward and went down to the Arabah.

19 The border continued to the side of Beth-hoglah northward; and the border ended at the north bay of the Salt Sea, at the south end of the Jordan. This was the south border.

20 Moreover, the Jordan was its border on the east side. This was the inheritance of the sons of Benjamin, according to their families and according to its borders all around.

21 Now the cities of the tribe of the sons of Benjamin according to their families were Jericho and Beth-hoglah and Emek-keziz,

22 and Beth-arabah and Zemaraim and Bethel,

23 and Avvim and Parah and Ophrah,

24 and Chephar-ammoni and Ophni and Geba; twelve cities with their villages.

25 Gibeon and Ramah and Beeroth,

26 and Mizpeh and Chephirah and Mozah,

Joshua
Chapter 18

27 and Rekem and Irpeel and Taralah,

28 and Zelah, Haeleph and the Jebusite (that is, Jerusalem), Gibeah, Kiriath; fourteen cities with their villages. This is the inheritance of the sons of Benjamin according to their families.

Joshua
Chapter 18

Joshua
Chapter 19

JOSHUA 19
OBSERVATION WORKSHEET

Chapter Theme _____

THEN the second lot fell to Simeon, to the tribe of the sons of Simeon according to their families, and their inheritance was in the midst of the inheritance of the sons of Judah.

2 So they had as their inheritance Beersheba or Sheba and Moladah,

3 and Hazar-shual and Balah and Ezem,

4 and Eltolad and Bethul and Hormah,

5 and Ziklag and Beth-marcaboth and Hazar-susah,

6 and Beth-lebaoth and Sharuhen; thirteen cities with their villages;

7 Ain, Rimmon and Ether and Ashan; four cities with their villages;

8 and all the villages which were around these cities as far as Baalath-beer, Ramah of the Negev. This was the inheritance of the tribe of the sons of Simeon according to their families.

9 The inheritance of the sons of Simeon was taken from the portion of the sons of Judah, for the share of the sons of Judah was too large for them; so the sons of Simeon received an inheritance in the midst of Judah's inheritance.

10 Now the third lot came up for the sons of Zebulun according to their families. And the territory of their inheritance was as far as Sarid.

11 Then their border went up to the west and to Maralah, it then touched Dabbesheth and reached to the brook that is before Jokneam.

12 Then it turned from Sarid to the east toward the sunrise as far as the border of Chisloth-tabor, and it proceeded to Daberath and up to Japhia.

13 From there it continued eastward toward the sunrise to Gath-hepher, to Eth-kazin, and it proceeded to Rimmon which stretches to Neah.

14 The border circled around it on the north to Hannathon, and it ended at the valley of Iphtahel.

15 Included also were Kattah and Nahalal and Shimron and Idalah and Bethlehem; twelve cities with their villages.

© 2008 Precept Ministries International

Joshua
Chapter 19

16 This was the inheritance of the sons of Zebulun according to their families, these cities with their villages.

17 The fourth lot fell to Issachar, to the sons of Issachar according to their families.

18 Their territory was to Jezreel and included Chesulloth and Shunem,

19 and Hapharaim and Shion and Anaharath,

20 and Rabbith and Kishion and Ebez,

21 and Remeth and En-gannim and En-haddah and Beth-pazzez.

22 The border reached to Tabor and Shahazumah and Beth-shemesh, and their border ended at the Jordan; sixteen cities with their villages.

23 This was the inheritance of the tribe of the sons of Issachar according to their families, the cities with their villages.

24 Now the fifth lot fell to the tribe of the sons of Asher according to their families.

25 Their territory was Helkath and Hali and Beten and Achshaph,

26 and Allammelech and Amad and Mishal; and it reached to Carmel on the west and to Shihor-libnath.

27 It turned toward the east to Beth-dagon and reached to Zebulun, and to the valley of Iphtahel northward to Beth-emek and Neiel; then it proceeded on north to Cabul,

28 and Ebron and Rehob and Hammon and Kanah, as far as Great Sidon.

29 The border turned to Ramah and to the fortified city of Tyre; then the border turned to Hosah, and it ended at the sea by the region of Achzib.

30 Included also were Ummah, and Aphek and Rehob; twenty-two cities with their villages.

31 This was the inheritance of the tribe of the sons of Asher according to their families, these cities with their villages.

32 The sixth lot fell to the sons of Naphtali; to the sons of Naphtali according to their families.

33 Their border was from Heleph, from the oak in Zaanannim and Adami- nekeb and Jabneel, as far as Lakkum, and it ended at the Jordan.

34 Then the border turned westward to Aznoth-tabor and proceeded from there to Hukkok; and it reached to Zebulun on the south and touched Asher on the west, and to Judah at the Jordan toward the east.

Joshua
Chapter 19

35 The fortified cities were Ziddim, Zer and Hammath, Rakkath and Chinnereth,

36 and Adamah and Ramah and Hazor,

37 and Kedesh and Edrei and En-hazor,

38 and Yiron and Migdal-el, Horem and Beth-anath and Beth-shemesh; nineteen cities with their villages.

39 This was the inheritance of the tribe of the sons of Naphtali according to their families, the cities with their villages.

40 The seventh lot fell to the tribe of the sons of Dan according to their families.

41 The territory of their inheritance was Zorah and Eshtaol and Ir-shemesh,

42 and Shaalabbin and Aijalon and Ithlah,

43 and Elon and Timnah and Ekron,

44 and Eltekeh and Gibbethon and Baalath,

45 and Jehud and Bene-berak and Gath-rimmon,

46 and Me-jarkon and Rakkon, with the territory over against Joppa.

47 The territory of the sons of Dan proceeded beyond them; for the sons of Dan went up and fought with Leshem and captured it. Then they struck it with the edge of the sword and possessed it and settled in it; and they called Leshem Dan after the name of Dan their father.

48 This was the inheritance of the tribe of the sons of Dan according to their families, these cities with their villages.

49 When they finished apportioning the land for inheritance by its borders, the sons of Israel gave an inheritance in their midst to Joshua the son of Nun.

50 In accordance with the command of the LORD they gave him the city for which he asked, Timnath-serah in the hill country of Ephraim. So he built the city and settled in it.

51 These are the inheritances which Eleazar the priest, and Joshua the son of Nun, and the heads of the households of the tribes of the sons of Israel distributed by lot in Shiloh before the LORD at the doorway of the tent of meeting. So they finished dividing the land.

© 2008 Precept Ministries International

Joshua
Chapter 19

JOSHUA 20
OBSERVATION WORKSHEET

Chapter Theme _____

THEN the LORD spoke to Joshua, saying,

2 "Speak to the sons of Israel, saying, 'Designate the cities of refuge, of which I spoke to you through Moses,

3 that the manslayer who kills any person unintentionally, without pre- meditation, may flee there, and they shall become your refuge from the avenger of blood.

4 'He shall flee to one of these cities, and shall stand at the entrance of the gate of the city and state his case in the hearing of the elders of that city; and they shall take him into the city to them and give him a place, so that he may dwell among them.

5 'Now if the avenger of blood pursues him, then they shall not deliver the manslayer into his hand, because he struck his neighbor without premed- itation and did not hate him beforehand.

6 'He shall dwell in that city until he stands before the congregation for judgment, un- til the death of the one who is high priest in those days. Then the manslayer shall return to his own city and to his own house, to the city from which he fled.'"

7 So they set apart Kedesh in Galilee in the hill country of Naphtali and Shechem in the hill country of Ephraim, and Kiriath-arba (that is, Hebron) in the hill country of Judah.

8 Beyond the Jordan east of Jericho, they designated Bezer in the wilderness on the plain from the tribe of Reuben, and Ramoth in Gilead from the tribe of Gad, and Golan in Bashan from the tribe of Manasseh.

9 These were the appointed cities for all the sons of Israel and for the stranger who so- journs among them, that whoever kills any person unintentionally may flee there, and not die by the hand of the avenger of blood until he stands before the congre- gation.

Joshua
Chapter 20

Joshua
Chapter 21

JOSHUA 21
OBSERVATION WORKSHEET

Chapter Theme _____

THEN the heads of households of the Levites approached Eleazar the priest, and Joshua the son of Nun, and the heads of households of the tribes of the sons of Israel.

2 They spoke to them at Shiloh in the land of Canaan, saying, "The LORD commanded through Moses to give us cities to live in, with their pasture lands for our cattle."

3 So the sons of Israel gave the Levites from their inheritance these cities with their pasture lands, according to the command of the LORD.

4 Then the lot came out for the families of the Kohathites. And the sons of Aaron the priest, who were of the Levites, received thirteen cities by lot from the tribe of Judah and from the tribe of the Simeonites and from the tribe of Benjamin.

5 The rest of the sons of Kohath received ten cities by lot from the families of the tribe of Ephraim and from the tribe of Dan and from the half-tribe of Manasseh.

6 The sons of Gershon received thirteen cities by lot from the families of the tribe of Issachar and from the tribe of Asher and from the tribe of Naphtali and from the half-tribe of Manasseh in Bashan.

7 The sons of Merari according to their families received twelve cities from the tribe of Reuben and from the tribe of Gad and from the tribe of Zebulun.

8 Now the sons of Israel gave by lot to the Levites these cities with their pasture lands, as the LORD had commanded through Moses.

9 They gave these cities which are here mentioned by name from the tribe of the sons of Judah and from the tribe of the sons of Simeon;

10 and they were for the sons of Aaron, one of the families of the Kohathites, of the sons of Levi, for the lot was theirs first.

11 Thus they gave them Kiriath-arba, Arba being the father of Anak (that is, Hebron), in the hill country of Judah, with its surrounding pasture lands.

12 But the fields of the city and its villages they gave to Caleb the son of Jephunneh as his possession.

© 2008 Precept Ministries International

Joshua
Chapter 21

13 So to the sons of Aaron the priest they gave Hebron, the city of refuge for the manslayer, with its pasture lands, and Libnah with its pasture lands,

14 and Jattir with its pasture lands and Eshtemoa with its pasture lands,

15 and Holon with its pasture lands and Debir with its pasture lands,

16 and Ain with its pasture lands and Juttah with its pasture lands and Beth-shemesh with its pasture lands; nine cities from these two tribes.

17 From the tribe of Benjamin, Gibeon with its pasture lands, Geba with its pasture lands,

18 Anathoth with its pasture lands and Almon with its pasture lands; four cities.

19 All the cities of the sons of Aaron, the priests, were thirteen cities with their pasture lands.

20 Then the cities from the tribe of Ephraim were allotted to the families of the sons of Kohath, the Levites, even to the rest of the sons of Kohath.

21 They gave them Shechem, the city of refuge for the manslayer, with its pasture lands, in the hill country of Ephraim, and Gezer with its pasture lands,

22 and Kibzaim with its pasture lands and Beth-horon with its pasture lands; four cities.

23 From the tribe of Dan, Elteke with its pasture lands, Gibbethon with its pasture lands,

24 Aijalon with its pasture lands, Gath-rimmon with its pasture lands; four cities.

25 From the half-tribe of Manasseh, they allotted Taanach with its pasture lands and Gath-rimmon with its pasture lands; two cities.

26 All the cities with their pasture lands for the families of the rest of the sons of Kohath were ten.

27 To the sons of Gershon, one of the families of the Levites, from the half-tribe of Manasseh, they gave Golan in Bashan, the city of refuge for the manslayer, with its pasture lands, and Be-eshterah with its pasture lands; two cities.

28 From the tribe of Issachar, they gave Kishion with its pasture lands, Daberath with its pasture lands,

29 Jarmuth with its pasture lands, En-gannim with its pasture lands; four cities.

30 From the tribe of Asher, they gave Mishal with its pasture lands, Abdon with its pasture lands,

Joshua
Chapter 21

31 Helkath with its pasture lands and Rehob with its pasture lands; four cities.

32 From the tribe of Naphtali, they gave Kedesh in Galilee, the city of refuge for the manslayer, with its pasture lands and Hammoth-dor with its pasture lands and Kartan with its pasture lands; three cities.

33 All the cities of the Gershonites according to their families were thirteen cities with their pasture lands.

34 To the families of the sons of Merari, the rest of the Levites, they gave from the tribe of Zebulun, Jokneam with its pasture lands and Kartah with its pasture lands.

35 Dimnah with its pasture lands, Nahalal with its pasture lands; four cities.

36 From the tribe of Reuben, they gave Bezer with its pasture lands and Jahaz with its pasture lands,

37 Kedemoth with its pasture lands and Mephaath with its pasture lands; four cities.

38 From the tribe of Gad, they gave Ramoth in Gilead, the city of refuge for the manslayer, with its pasture lands and Mahanaim with its pasture lands,

39 Heshbon with its pasture lands, Jazer with its pasture lands; four cities in all.

40 All these were the cities of the sons of Merari according to their families, the rest of the families of the Levites; and their lot was twelve cities.

41 All the cities of the Levites in the midst of the possession of the sons of Israel were forty-eight cities with their pasture lands.

42 These cities each had its surrounding pasture lands; thus it was with all these cities.

43 So the LORD gave Israel all the land which He had sworn to give to their fathers, and they possessed it and lived in it.

44 And the LORD gave them rest on every side, according to all that He had sworn to their fathers, and no one of all their enemies stood before them; the LORD gave all their enemies into their hand.

45 Not one of the good promises which the LORD had made to the house of Israel failed; all came to pass.

© 2008 Precept Ministries International

Joshua
Chapter 21

Joshua
Chapter 22

JOSHUA 22
OBSERVATION WORKSHEET

Chapter Theme _____

THEN Joshua summoned the Reubenites and the Gadites and the half-tribe of Manasseh,

2 and said to them, "You have kept all that Moses the servant of the LORD commanded you, and have listened to my voice in all that I commanded you.

3 "You have not forsaken your brothers these many days to this day, but have kept the charge of the commandment of the LORD your God.

4 "And now the LORD your God has given rest to your brothers, as He spoke to them; therefore turn now and go to your tents, to the land of your possession, which Moses the servant of the LORD gave you beyond the Jordan.

5 "Only be very careful to observe the commandment and the law which Moses the servant of the LORD commanded you, to love the LORD your God and walk in all His ways and keep His commandments and hold fast to Him and serve Him with all your heart and with all your soul."

6 So Joshua blessed them and sent them away, and they went to their tents.

7 Now to the one half-tribe of Manasseh Moses had given a possession in Bashan, but to the other half Joshua gave a possession among their brothers westward beyond the Jordan. So when Joshua sent them away to their tents, he blessed them,

8 and said to them, "Return to your tents with great riches and with very much livestock, with silver, gold, bronze, iron, and with very many clothes; divide the spoil of your enemies with your brothers."

9 The sons of Reuben and the sons of Gad and the half-tribe of Manasseh returned home and departed from the sons of Israel at Shiloh which is in the land of Canaan, to go to the land of Gilead, to the land of their possession which they had possessed, according to the command of the LORD through Moses.

10 When they came to the region of the Jordan which is in the land of Canaan, the sons of Reuben and the sons of Gad and the half-tribe of Manasseh built an altar there by the Jordan, a large altar in appearance.

© 2008 Precept Ministries International

Joshua
Chapter 22

11 And the sons of Israel heard it said, "Behold, the sons of Reuben and the sons of Gad and the half-tribe of Manasseh have built an altar at the frontier of the land of Canaan, in the region of the Jordan, on the side belonging to the sons of Israel."

12 When the sons of Israel heard of it, the whole congregation of the sons of Israel gathered themselves at Shiloh to go up against them in war.

13 Then the sons of Israel sent to the sons of Reuben and to the sons of Gad and to the half-tribe of Manasseh, into the land of Gilead, Phinehas the son of Eleazar the priest,

14 and with him ten chiefs, one chief for each father's household from each of the tribes of Israel; and each one of them was the head of his father's household among the thousands of Israel.

15 They came to the sons of Reuben and to the sons of Gad and to the half-tribe of Manasseh, to the land of Gilead, and they spoke with them saying,

16 "Thus says the whole congregation of the LORD, 'What is this unfaithful act which you have committed against the God of Israel, turning away from following the LORD this day, by building yourselves an altar, to rebel against the LORD this day?

17 'Is not the iniquity of Peor enough for us, from which we have not cleansed ourselves to this day, although a plague came on the congregation of the LORD,

18 that you must turn away this day from following the LORD? If you rebel against the LORD today, He will be angry with the whole congregation of Israel tomorrow.

19 'If, however, the land of your possession is unclean, then cross into the land of the possession of the LORD, where the LORD's tabernacle stands, and take possession among us. Only do not rebel against the LORD, or rebel against us by building an altar for yourselves, besides the altar of the LORD our God.

20 'Did not Achan the son of Zerah act unfaithfully in the things under the ban, and wrath fall on all the congregation of Israel? And that man did not perish alone in his iniquity.'"

21 Then the sons of Reuben and the sons of Gad and the half-tribe of Manasseh answered and spoke to the heads of the families of Israel.

22 "The Mighty One, God, the LORD, the Mighty One, God, the LORD! He knows,

Joshua
Chapter 22

and may Israel itself know. If it was in rebellion, or if in an unfaithful act against the LORD do not save us this day!

23 "If we have built us an altar to turn away from following the LORD, or if to offer a burnt offering or grain offering on it, or if to offer sacrifices of peace offerings on it, may the LORD Himself require it.

24 "But truly we have done this out of concern, for a reason, saying, 'In time to come your sons may say to our sons, "What have you to do with the LORD, the God of Israel?

25 "For the LORD has made the Jordan a border between us and you, you sons of Reuben and sons of Gad; you have no portion in the LORD." So your sons may make our sons stop fearing the LORD.'

26 "Therefore we said, 'Let us build an altar, not for burnt offering or for sacrifice;

27 rather it shall be a witness between us and you and between our generations after us, that we are to perform the service of the LORD before Him with our burnt offerings, and with our sacrifices and with our peace offerings, so that your sons will not say to our sons in time to come, "You have no portion in the LORD."'

28 "Therefore we said, 'It shall also come about if they say this to us or to our generations in time to come, then we shall say, "See the copy of the altar of the LORD which our fathers made, not for burnt offering or for sacrifice; rather it is a witness between us and you."'

29 "Far be it from us that we should rebel against the LORD and turn away from following the LORD this day, by building an altar for burnt offering, for grain offering or for sacrifice, besides the altar of the LORD our God which is before His tabernacle."

30 So when Phinehas the priest and the leaders of the congregation, even the heads of the families of Israel who were with him, heard the words which the sons of Reuben and the sons of Gad and the sons of Manasseh spoke, it pleased them.

31 And Phinehas the son of Eleazar the priest said to the sons of Reuben and to the sons of Gad and to the sons of Manasseh, "Today we know that the LORD is in our midst, because you have not committed this unfaithful act against the LORD; now you have delivered the sons of Israel from the hand of the LORD."

32 Then Phinehas the son of Eleazar the priest and the leaders returned from the sons

Joshua
Chapter 22

of Reuben and from the sons of Gad, from the land of Gilead to the land of Canaan, to the sons of Israel, and brought back word to them.

33 The word pleased the sons of Israel, and the sons of Israel blessed God; and they did not speak of going up against them in war to destroy the land in which the sons of Reuben and the sons of Gad were living.

34 The sons of Reuben and the sons of Gad called the altar Witness; "For," they said, "it is a witness between us that the LORD is God."

Joshua
Chapter 23

JOSHUA 23
OBSERVATION WORKSHEET

Chapter Theme _____

NOW it came about after many days, when the LORD had given rest to Israel from all their enemies on every side, and Joshua was old, advanced in years,

2   that Joshua called for all Israel, for their elders and their heads and their judges and their officers, and said to them, "I am old, advanced in years.

3   "And you have seen all that the LORD your God has done to all these nations because of you, for the LORD your God is He who has been fighting for you.

4   "See, I have apportioned to you these nations which remain as an inheritance for your tribes, with all the nations which I have cut off, from the Jordan even to the Great Sea toward the setting of the sun.

5   "The LORD your God, He will thrust them out from before you and drive them from before you; and you will possess their land, just as the LORD your God promised you.

6   "Be very firm, then, to keep and do all that is written in the book of the law of Moses, so that you may not turn aside from it to the right hand or to the left,

7   so that you will not associate with these nations, these which remain among you, or mention the name of their gods, or make anyone swear by them, or serve them, or bow down to them.

8   "But you are to cling to the LORD your God, as you have done to this day.

9   "For the LORD has driven out great and strong nations from before you; and as for you, no man has stood before you to this day.

10 "One of your men puts to flight a thousand, for the LORD your God is He who fights for you, just as He promised you.

11 "So take diligent heed to yourselves to love the LORD your God.

12 "For if you ever go back and cling to the rest of these nations, these which remain among you, and intermarry with them, so that you associate with them and they with you,

13 know with certainty that the LORD your God will not continue to drive these na-

© 2008 Precept Ministries International

Joshua
Chapter 23

tions out from before you; but they will be a snare and a trap to you, and a whip on your sides and thorns in your eyes, until you perish from off this good land which the LORD your God has given you.

14 "Now behold, today I am going the way of all the earth, and you know in all your hearts and in all your souls that not one word of all the good words which the LORD your God spoke concerning you has failed; all have been fulfilled for you, not one of them has failed.

15 "It shall come about that just as all the good words which the LORD your God spoke to you have come upon you, so the LORD will bring upon you all the threats, until He has destroyed you from off this good land which the LORD your God has given you.

16 "When you transgress the covenant of the LORD your God, which He commanded you, and go and serve other gods and bow down to them, then the anger of the LORD will burn against you, and you will perish quickly from off the good land which He has given you."

Joshua
Chapter 24

JOSHUA 24
OBSERVATION WORKSHEET

Chapter Theme _____

THEN Joshua gathered all the tribes of Israel to Shechem, and called for the elders of Israel and for their heads and their judges and their officers; and they presented themselves before God.

2 Joshua said to all the people, "Thus says the LORD, the God of Israel, 'From ancient times your fathers lived beyond the River, namely, Terah, the father of Abraham and the father of Nahor, and they served other gods.

3 'Then I took your father Abraham from beyond the River, and led him through all the land of Canaan, and multiplied his descendants and gave him Isaac.

4 'To Isaac I gave Jacob and Esau, and to Esau I gave Mount Seir to possess it; but Jacob and his sons went down to Egypt.

5 'Then I sent Moses and Aaron, and I plagued Egypt by what I did in its midst; and afterward I brought you out.

6 'I brought your fathers out of Egypt, and you came to the sea; and Egypt pursued your fathers with chariots and horsemen to the Red Sea.

7 'But when they cried out to the LORD, He put darkness between you and the Egyptians, and brought the sea upon them and covered them; and your own eyes saw what I did in Egypt. And you lived in the wilderness for a long time.

8 'Then I brought you into the land of the Amorites who lived beyond the Jordan, and they fought with you; and I gave them into your hand, and you took possession of their land when I destroyed them before you.

9 'Then Balak the son of Zippor, king of Moab, arose and fought against Israel, and he sent and summoned Balaam the son of Beor to curse you.

10 'But I was not willing to listen to Balaam. So he had to bless you, and I delivered you from his hand.

11 'You crossed the Jordan and came to Jericho; and the citizens of Jericho fought against you, and the Amorite and the Perizzite and the Canaanite and the Hittite

© 2008 Precept Ministries International

Joshua
Chapter 24

and the Girgashite, the Hivite and the Jebusite. Thus I gave them into your hand.

12 'Then I sent the hornet before you and it drove out the two kings of the Amorites from before you, but not by your sword or your bow.

13 'I gave you a land on which you had not labored, and cities which you had not built, and you have lived in them; you are eating of vineyards and olive groves which you did not plant.'

14 "Now, therefore, fear the LORD and serve Him in sincerity and truth; and put away the gods which your fathers served beyond the River and in Egypt, and serve the LORD.

15 "If it is disagreeable in your sight to serve the LORD, choose for yourselves today whom you will serve: whether the gods which your fathers served which were beyond the River, or the gods of the Amorites in whose land you are living; but as for me and my house, we will serve the LORD."

16 The people answered and said, "Far be it from us that we should forsake the LORD to serve other gods;

17 for the LORD our God is He who brought us and our fathers up out of the land of Egypt, from the house of bondage, and who did these great signs in our sight and preserved us through all the way in which we went and among all the peoples through whose midst we passed.

18 "The LORD drove out from before us all the peoples, even the Amorites who lived in the land. We also will serve the LORD, for He is our God."

19 Then Joshua said to the people, "You will not be able to serve the LORD, for He is a holy God. He is a jealous God; He will not forgive your transgression or your sins.

20 "If you forsake the LORD and serve foreign gods, then He will turn and do you harm and consume you after He has done good to you."

21 The people said to Joshua, "No, but we will serve the LORD."

22 Joshua said to the people, "You are witnesses against yourselves that you have chosen for yourselves the LORD, to serve Him." And they said, "We are witnesses."

23 "Now therefore, put away the foreign gods which are in your midst, and incline your hearts to the LORD, the God of Israel."

24 The people said to Joshua, "We will serve the LORD our God and we will obey His

Joshua
Chapter 24

voice."

25 So Joshua made a covenant with the people that day, and made for them a statute and an ordinance in Shechem.

26 And Joshua wrote these words in the book of the law of God; and he took a large stone and set it up there under the oak that was by the sanctuary of the LORD.

27 Joshua said to all the people, "Behold, this stone shall be for a witness against us, for it has heard all the words of the LORD which He spoke to us; thus it shall be for a witness against you, so that you do not deny your God."

28 Then Joshua dismissed the people, each to his inheritance.

29 It came about after these things that Joshua the son of Nun, the servant of the LORD, died, being one hundred and ten years old.

30 And they buried him in the territory of his inheritance in Timnath-serah, which is in the hill country of Ephraim, on the north of Mount Gaash.

31 Israel served the LORD all the days of Joshua and all the days of the elders who survived Joshua, and had known all the deeds of the LORD which He had done for Israel.

32 Now they buried the bones of Joseph, which the sons of Israel brought up from Egypt, at Shechem, in the piece of ground which Jacob had bought from the sons of Hamor the father of Shechem for one hundred pieces of money; and they became the inheritance of Joseph's sons.

33 And Eleazar the son of Aaron died; and they buried him at Gibeah of Phinehas his son, which was given him in the hill country of Ephraim.

Joshua
Chapter 24

AT A GLANCE CHART

Joshua

BOOK THEME:

SEGMENT DIVISIONS	CHAPTER THEMES
	1
	2
	3
	4
	5
	6
	7
	8
	9
	10
	11
	12
	13
	14
	15
	16
	17
	18
	19
	20
	21
	22
	23
	24

Joshua

OCCUPYING THE LAND

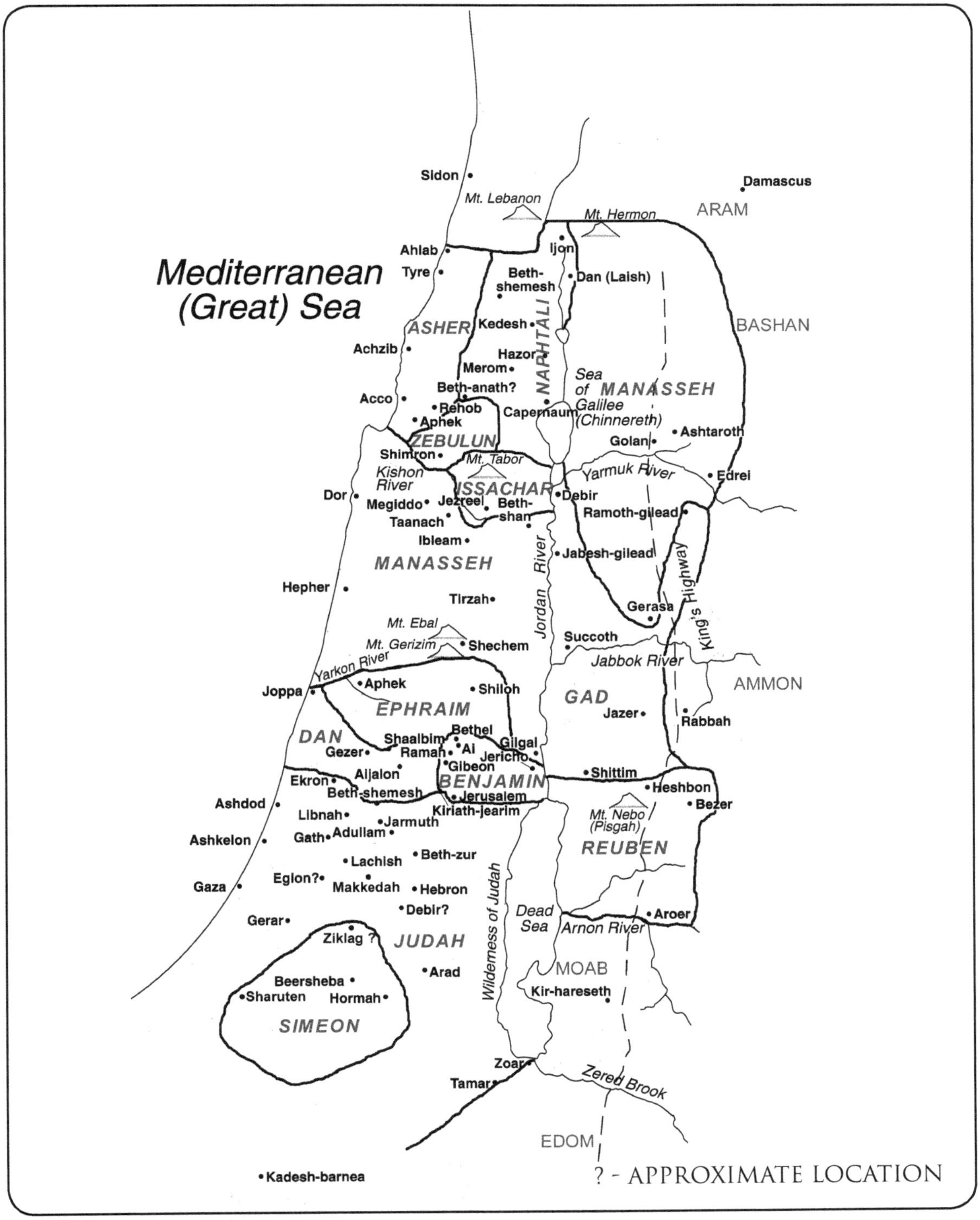

? - APPROXIMATE LOCATION

Joshua

Joshua

CONQUERING THE LAND

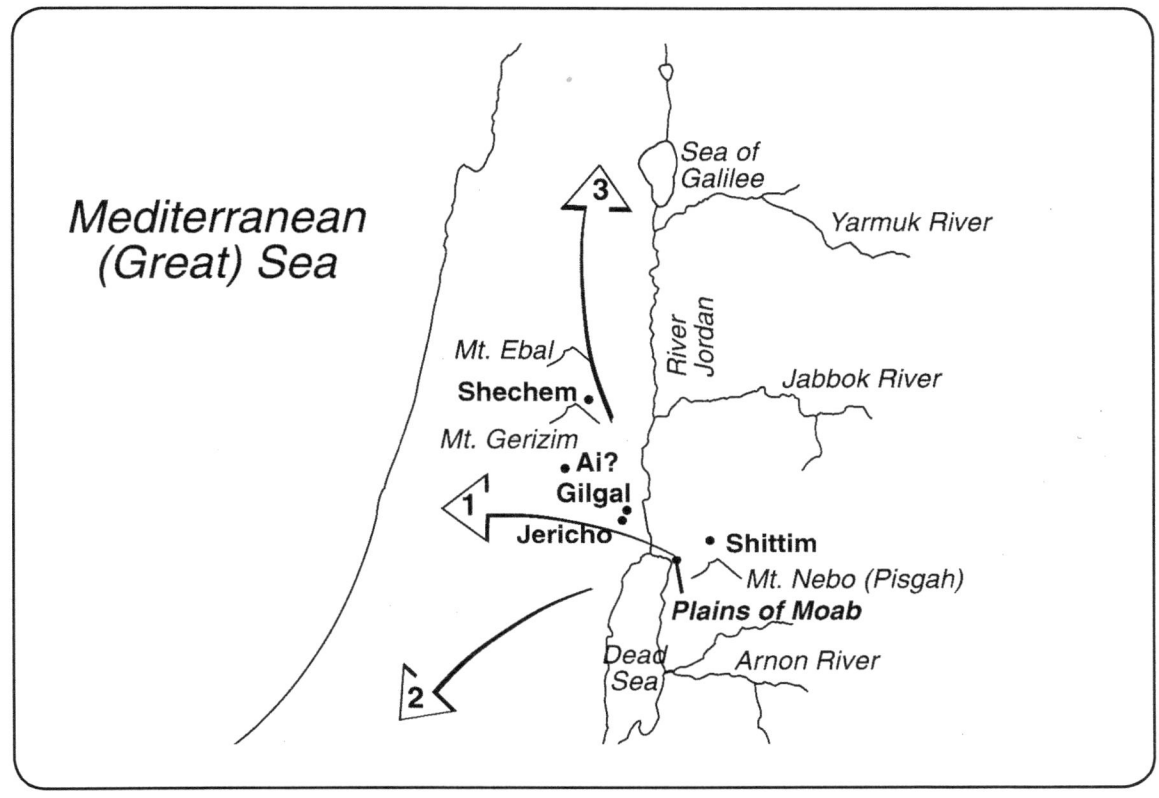

www.ingramcontent.com/pod-product-compliance
Lightning Source LLC
Chambersburg PA
CBHW062126160426
43191CB00013B/2214